Roots of Pentecostal Belief

SPIRITUAL HERITAGE OF TODAY'S PENTECOSTAL

JOHN W. WYCKOFF

Radiant Life
1445 North Boonville Avenue
Springfield, MO 65802-1894
02-0132

STAFF

National Director: Arlyn R. Pember
Editor in Chief: John T. Maempa
Adult Projects Editor: Paul W. Smith
Product Coordinator: Robert L. Walden
Designers: Steve Lopez, Craig W. Schutt
Cover Design: Craig W. Schutt

All photos courtesy Flower Pentecostal Heritage Center.
Cover art by Gary Locke, courtesy Flower Pentecostal Heritage Center.

A Leader's Guide for individual or group study with this book is available
(order number 02-0232) 088243-232-X

Contents

WELCOME TO THE

SPIRITUAL *Discovery* SERIES

We are glad you have chosen to study with us. We believe the discoveries you make through the use of the *Spiritual Discovery Series* will positively impact your life.

The *Spiritual Discovery Series* will challenge the user to ask questions of the biblical text, discover principles from the text, and make personal application of those truths. The Bible is the text. This guide is a tool for study.

The *Spiritual Discovery Series* is designed for use in either individual or group settings. Individuals will be excited by the discoveries made possible through a structured inductive study. Sunday School classes and other groups will find the *Spiritual Discovery Series* a valuable tool for promoting enlightened discussions centered on biblical truth.

HOW TO USE THIS STUDY GUIDE

1 **Pray before beginning each study session.** Ask the Holy Spirit to illuminate your mind.

2 **Choose a translation of the Bible which you trust and can understand.** It will be helpful to have more than one translation available to aid your understanding of the biblical text.

3 **The Bible is your primary text.** Avoid using commentaries or reference books until after completing your own study. Reference works are best used to confirm your findings. On occasion, the study guide will direct you to use reference material. This is done when special insights are necessary for proper interpretation.

4 **Read the assigned biblical text at least twice before answering any questions.** This will provide an overview and focus on God's Word.

5 **Concentrate on the biblical passage which you are studying.** It is tempting to jump from one passage of Scripture to another in an attempt to make spiritual connections.

6 **Seek tangible ways to apply the principles gleaned from each study.** Bible study should never result in "head knowledge" alone. Bible study should lead to action.

REFORMATION:
AUTHORITY OF SCRIPTURE

The Pentecostal experience is wonderful and also essential. Likewise, the teachings of gifted Pentecostal leaders are also important. But Church history reveals that when the experiences and doctrines of men become the final authority and standard, the Church is weakened and destroyed; and individuals are misguided and lost. This is why we begin this study by seeing why Pentecostals hold so strongly to the final authority of Scripture.

In the 16th century, Martin Luther and other Reformers who followed him emphasized the importance of making the Bible the final authority for Christian doctrine and practice. Early in the 20th century, when the Pentecostal Movement began, Pentecostals ardently embraced this Reformation principle as well.

THE BIBLE IS GOD'S WORD

In 2 Timothy 3:14-17, the apostle Paul was writing to Timothy, his fellow coworker. In verse 14, Paul reminded young Timothy that he knew about a sure source of understanding and wisdom. In fact, Timothy had known about this sure source and had been convinced of its validity from his earliest childhood. Paul then admonished Timothy to continue to live his life and perform his ministry according to this sure source of understanding and wisdom.

1. In 2 Timothy 3:15, Paul identified the source that is able to make you wise regarding "salvation through faith which is in Christ Jesus." What is this source?

_____

2. From 2 Timothy 3:16, list the four things for which Paul stated Scripture is profitable or useful.

_____

_____

_____

_____

3. In the very first part of 2 Timothy 3:16, what did Paul say about the origin and character of Scripture that makes it profitable or useful?

_____

_____

_____

Paul concluded this passage by pointing out that, if Timothy would continue to follow the standard of understanding and wisdom set forth in Scripture, he would accomplish what God desired for him to accomplish.

You can claim this promise for yourself. If you learn and follow the truth of Scripture, you will become all that God wants you to be.

In 2 Peter 1:19-21, the apostle Peter told his readers that God's unchanging prophetic Word (referring to the written Word of God, the Bible), is a standard that cannot be altered by men's ideas and understandings. It is a "sure word" from God.

Peter stated, "no prophecy of Scripture is a matter of one's own interpretation" (2 Peter 1:20). This means that no one has the right to make God's prophetic Word say or mean just anything they think or desire.

✎ 4. According to 2 Peter 1:21, what did Peter say about the origin of Scripture that keeps you from giving your own meaning to it?

_____

_____

_____

✎ 5. In your own words, state what Peter's illustration of "a lamp shining in a dark place" in 2 Peter 1:19 says about the usefulness and value of God's Word to you.

_____

_____

_____

_____

Second Peter 1:21 gives significant insight into how Scripture was produced. Look at this verse closely as you answer the next two questions.

✎ 6. Does 2 Peter 1:21 indicate that humans were involved in producing God's Word? Explain your answer.

_____

_____

_____

_____

✎ 7. According to 2 Peter 1:21, who did Peter say is the ultimate source of prophecy?

_____

The production of Scripture was a cooperative effort involving both human instruments (human authors) and divine agency (the Holy Spirit). The result was a sure word from God that always provides an understandable standard by which all men can know the will of God—the Bible.

The church at Colossae was one of several churches established in the Roman province of Asia during Paul's third missionary journey (Colossians 2:8-10). Some time after Paul left the area, false teachings based on Greek philosophy crept into the church. These false teachings were contrary to an accurate understanding of the divine nature of Christ. Paul wrote the Epistle to the Colossians to correct these false teachings.

Considering the whole context of Colossians, verse 8 does not mean Paul is opposed to or wants to ignore all philosophy, tradition, and principles. He knows we all have a philosophy of life, we all live with tradition, and we all embrace principles that guide our lives.

8a. Look closely at Colossians 2:8. To what specific kind of philosophy is Paul opposed?

_____

_____

8b. To what particular kind of tradition is Paul opposed?

_____

8c. To what certain kind of principles is Paul opposed?

_____

_____

9. At the end of Colossians 2:8, Paul stated that our philosophy, tradition, and principles should be according to what (or whom)?

_____

10. Colossians 2:9,10 says that "all the fullness of Deity" is expressed in whom?

_____

11. What do you presently have in your hands that provides you with authoritative understanding of Jesus? Who helps you know when your experiences, doctrines, and practices are according to Him?

_____

_____

_____

_____

THE BIBLE THROUGH THE AGES

First Century To Reformation Era

During the first century of the Church the apostles were recognized as authoritative teachers on the significance of the "Christ Event" in light of the Old Testament Scriptures. (By the Christ Event we mean the incarnation, ministry, death, resurrection, and ascension of Jesus.) At first, the "apostles' teaching" (Acts 2:42) was given, passed along, and preserved orally. However, by the inspiration of the Holy Spirit, the apostles and their closest associates soon wrote down their understanding and applications of the Christ Event for the rapidly growing body of believers.

As time passed and the Church continued to expand, those who knew the oral traditions became less available. Believers increasingly relied upon the written form of the apostles' teachings. These writings were copied and passed from one community of believers to another as the Church exploded through the Roman Empire and beyond. The written word was held to be standard for knowing what should be taught and practiced among believers everywhere. They were eventually collected together into what became known as the New Testament **canon**.

✎ 12. The word canon is a Latin term. Circle two of the following words that give the basic meaning of the term canon. (If necessary, get help by looking up canon in a standard dictionary.)

BOOKS   COLLECTION   CRITERION   STANDARD

✎ 13. What does the basic meaning of the term canon tell you about how the Early Church viewed the New Testament writings?

_____

_____

Immediately following the first century, believers continued to regard the teachings of the apostles as authoritative. In order to make the Scripture relevant and applicable in many places and various situations, the Church progressively developed a large body of teachings. Paul's statement in 2 Timothy 3:16 indicates that this was appropriate and necessary.

Unfortunately, over the following centuries, three things occurred relative to these Church teachings. First, they eventually included numerous doctrines and practices that were not in keeping with the teachings of the New Testament. Second, during the Medieval Period (A.D. 400-1500), when issues were raised about Church traditions that varied from the teachings of Scripture, hierarchal Church leaders held that the large body of Church traditions was the ultimate authority, rather than Scripture. Third, these leaders held that by virtue of their position in the Church, they were the sole, authoritative interpreters of both Church tradition and Scripture.

14. Again, look at Peter's warning in 2 Peter 1:19-21 and Paul's warning in Colossians 2:8-10. In your own words explain what went wrong during the Medieval Period.

_____

_____

_____

_____

Because of the teachings of the Church during Medieval times, the principle of Scripture's final authority was not understood for many centuries. Many people sincerely believed that God was giving new authoritative teachings in each succeeding generation of the Church.

15. Note the obvious problem by thinking about your response to the following statement: Is it possible for the religious teachings, even the supposed "Christian" teachings, of an individual or group of individuals, to be contrary to the truth and will of God? Why?

_____

_____

_____

_____

16. Is there some unchanging, objective standard by which all religious teachings, "Christian" or otherwise, may be judged for their accuracy and validity?

_____

_____

_____

The Protestant Reformation of the 16th century supplied the answer to this all-important question. Martin Luther (1483-1546), and other Reformers such as John Calvin (1509-1564) asserted the principle of _Sola Scriptura_ (Latin for "Scripture alone").

They recognized that much of Church tradition was contrary to the clear teaching of Scripture and therefore it was incorrect. They rejected the doctrine of hierarchal Church authority and the ultimate authority of Church traditions over Scripture. They developed the doctrine that Scripture is the final authority and standard by which Christians must judge whether all teachings, practices, and experiences are correct.

Post-Reformation To Present

The principle that Scripture is the final rule of faith and practice was once again threatened by the rationalism and agnosticism of the Enlightenment Age (18th century). Many rationalists, deists, agnostics, and others came to believe that the Bible was simply a collection of ancient human writings of no unique, divine origins. They maintained that the Bible held no special authority and had little or no relevance to modern times.

✎17. Once again, consider Peter's warning in 2 Peter 1:19-21 and Paul's warning in Colossians 2:8-10. List your own observations about how these warnings apply to what happened during the Enlightenment Age.

_____

_____

_____

_____

_____

Fortunately, by the end of the 19th century, spiritual renewal movements such as the Second Great Awakening and the Holiness Movement had recaptured the great Reformation principle of *Sola Scriptura*. Participants in these movements insisted that while human authors were involved in the writing of Scripture, the ultimate author of all Scripture was the Holy Spirit. They insisted upon the inspiration and authority of what we now know as the Bible. (See 2 Timothy 3:14-17 and 2 Peter 1:19-21.)

Historically, the Pentecostal Movement flowed out of the Holiness Movement which occurred during the last half of the 19th century. Early Pentecostals at the beginning of the 20th century insisted on maintaining the "authority of the Scripture" principle that came to them from the Reformation and Holiness traditions. These early Pentecostals also insisted on the reality of personal experience with God—"born again" salvation, baptism in the Holy Spirit, accompanied by "speaking in tongues"(speaking in languages they had not learned through the power of the Holy Spirit), manifestation of spiritual gifts, and other spiritual experiences.

✎18. As you think about your response to the following statement, consider the great diversity and variety of possible religious or spiritual experiences among people. Is it possible for religious or spiritual experiences, even supposed "Christian" experiences, to be contrary to God's truth and will? Why?

_____

_____

_____

_____

✎ 19. Is there some unchanging, objective standard by which all religious and/or spiritual experiences may be judged for their validity, accuracy and appropriateness? What is that standard?

_____

_____

_____

Certainly early Pentecostals cherished their spiritual experiences. Their relationship with the living God began with a personal born-again experience. This was followed by the experience of baptism in the Holy Spirit with speaking in tongues. They often experienced divine healing and the manifestation of other spiritual gifts. But as significant as all of these experiences were, these early Pentecostals also recognized the necessity of judging the validity of all such experiences by the teachings of Scripture.

✎ 20. Is it possible for any Christian group, Pentecostal or otherwise, to develop doctrines and practices that are not in keeping with God's truth and will? How? What could be done to guard against this?

_____

_____

_____

_____

SUMMARY

The position that Scripture is authoritative and relevant for today is the centerpiece and beginning point of Pentecostal heritage. As important as spiritual experiences and Church traditions are, Scripture must be understood and adhered to as the final authority for faith and practice. Pentecostals believe that Scripture teaches this position. They, like other Christians, are indebted to the Reformation for realizing and developing this most basic truth. The "authority of Scripture" principle must be maintained in order for the Church to remain strong and effective and for individuals to be properly guided and established in all truth.

LET'S REVIEW

✎ 1. What Scripture passages confirm the idea that Scripture should be the final rule of faith and practice for Christians?

_____

✎ 2. Name the reform movement of the 16th century that identified and developed the principle that Scripture should be the final rule of faith and practice for Christians.

_____

✎ 3. Briefly restate the view of the Bible that came out of the Enlightenment Age and challenged the "authority of Scripture" principle.

_____

_____

_____

✎ 4. List the two spiritual renewal movements that helped to restore the "authority of Scripture" principle during the 19th century.

_____

_____

✎ 5. Why did participants in the 19th century movements say that the books in the Bible were not simply human writings?

_____

_____

✎ 6. In your own words, briefly restate the view of early Pentecostals regarding the role of Scripture in judging the validity, accuracy, and appropriateness of spiritual experiences.

_____

_____

_____

REFORMATION: SALVATION BY GRACE THROUGH FAITH

I n the previous study we learned the principle that Scripture is the ultimate standard for what Christians should believe and practice in their walk with God. We studied that principle first because it is the most fundamental element of Pentecostal heritage.

In this second study, we will learn the principle that personal salvation is by grace through faith alone and not by merit or works. Pentecostals believe this basic principle is clearly taught in Scripture.

FAITH OR WORKS?

During the Middle Ages (A.D. 400-1400), the Church progressively developed an elaborate system of "works righteousness." The Church taught that individuals could and, in fact, had to earn right standing before God by doing certain things within the framework of the Church establishment at that time.

Early in the 16th century, Martin Luther (1483-1546), after studying the Book of Romans, opposed the Church's doctrine of "works righteousness" and taught "the just shall live by faith" (Romans 1:17). Other Reformers like John Calvin (1509-1564) and Ulrich Zwingli (1484-1531) followed Luther's lead and helped make salvation by grace through faith a centerpiece of the Protestant Reformation. Later on in the early 20th century, the Pentecostal Movement—with its roots in the Reformation—also held this doctrine to be central to the full gospel.

Biblical Basis

Paul wrote the great letter of Romans to the church at Rome. He had not yet been there, but was hoping to go there soon. While he may have known a few of the Christians in Rome, there were many believers there that Paul did not personally know. Paul may have had a variety of reasons for writing this letter. But certainly among them was his desire for everyone in the church in Rome to know exactly what he believed concerning Jesus Christ and the gospel.

✎ 1. Romans 1:16,17 are classic verses on the way of salvation. In the first part of verse 16, what did Paul say is the power of God for salvation?

_____

_____

_____

✎ 2. Also in verse 16, Paul said there is only one way to salvation for everyone. However, what two groups of people did Paul especially identify?

_____

_____

✎ 3. In verse 17, Paul clearly stated the one and only way for anyone to obtain the righteousness of God (that is, right standing before God). How did Paul say that the righteous or just man becomes righteous or just?

_____

_____

_____

4. Read Ephesians 2:8,9. In these verses, the apostle Paul was very specific about how salvation is obtained and how it is not. What two things did Paul say are not sources of our salvation?

_____

_____

5. From the first part of Ephesians 2:8, restate what Paul said about how one *is* saved.

_____

_____

6. Who is it that gives us the "gift" of salvation by grace through faith?

_____

7. Read Acts 15:5,8-11. Look closely at the context of these verses and identify the two groups of believers that Peter was talking about.

_____

_____

8. In Acts 15:9, the writer Luke quoted Peter as saying that God makes no distinction between Jewish and Gentile believers. In Acts 15:9,11, what did Peter say about how they are "saved" or cleansed and brought into right relationship with God?

_____

_____

_____

9. In Romans 3:21 through 5:17, Paul expounded upon the idea of salvation by grace through faith. Read the entire section. In Romans 3:28 Paul declared that a man is justified by faith without or apart from the works of the Law. If works related to the God-given, holy Law do not avail to salvation, what would you say concerning the ability of any other kinds of good works to bring salvation?

_____

_____

_____

18

✎ 10. In Romans 4, what Bible character did Paul give as an example of one being justified by faith rather than works in Old Testament times?

_____

✎ 11. In Romans 5:1, what did Paul say is our benefit, even now, if we have been justified by faith?

_____

_____

Read James 2:14-24. At this point in our study, it is important for us to notice another important truth that is directly related to what we have been studying in the Scriptures above. The great truth, "by grace you have been saved through faith,...not as a result of works" (Ephesians 2:8,9), must be properly balanced with another great truth: Works are in fact directly related to true salvation. This is best seen in James 2:14-24.

Read these verses in James 2 with the truth of justification by faith fresh in your mind. At first, you may think they are contrary to what we have just studied above. If you do have such thoughts, you are not alone. Others have thought the same thing. After all, does not James clearly teach in verse 21 that Abraham was justified by works? Does he not say in verse 20 that faith without works is "dead" (KJV) or "useless" (NIV)? And, in verse 24, does not James plainly conclude that one is justified by works and not by faith alone?

✎ 12. Compare James 2:24 in several translations. Is the truth of justification by faith clearly seen in all of these translations? What differences did you find? If any, list them below.

_____

_____

More careful and thoughtful consideration reveals, however, that James was not contradicting the teachings of Paul as some have thought. James was simply saying that the kind of true faith that results in genuine salvation will, without exception, bring forth good works from the redeemed individual.

✎ 13. Carefully look at James 2:14. When James was speaking of one who does not have good works, was he saying that the individual: (A) really has true faith; or, (B) "claims" to have faith? Write your answer below, and give a reason for your answer.

_____

_____

_____

Read James 2:14 again. By the term "such faith" (NIV), James meant that faith that does not produce works—if it can be called "faith" at all—is not genuine saving faith.

14. Interestingly in James 2:21-23, the author highlighted the same Bible character that Paul used in Romans 4—Abraham. Look closely at the very last part of James 2:22. In your own words, restate what James said is the relationship between faith and works.

_____

_____

_____

_____

In other words, James was simply saying that faith comes first; but if it is genuine saving faith, it *will* be followed by obedience. In James' example, Abraham followed through by offering his son Isaac as a sacrifice to God.

15. Look again at Paul's teachings on the "faith" subject in Ephesians 2:8-10. In verses 8 and 9, Paul taught salvation by grace through faith, and not by works. However, what did he go on to also teach in verse 10?

_____

_____

_____

_____

Paul and James do not contradict each other. In Romans 4, when Paul used Abraham as an example—like James did—he noted that Abraham followed through in obedience. Read Romans 4:11,12 in which Paul taught the same relationship of faith to works that James taught in James 2:22.

16. In Romans 4:12, what particular "work" did Abraham follow through to do after he was justified by faith?

_____

Finally, look at Ephesians 4:1 and compare Paul's point with James' point in James 2:18. Would you agree that they are teaching the same truth? Genuine salvation that comes by faith, must be followed with righteous deeds. Thus, according to Ephesians 4:1, Paul also expected those who are saved by faith "to live a life worthy of the calling you have received" (NIV).

HISTORICAL PERSPECTIVE

First Century To Reformation Era

From the Book of Acts we learn what the first century Church and the apostles believed and practiced regarding the relationship of works and faith to salvation. When the issue of how individuals are saved arose in the first century Church, the apostles called a meeting in Jerusalem to discuss the matter. This meeting, often referred to as the First Council of the Church, or the Council of Jerusalem, is recorded in Acts 15.

✏ 17. Read Acts 15, especially focusing on verses 1-11. In these verses you will see what happened during the First Council of the Church and the conclusion that was reached. Record your findings below.

_____

_____

_____

_____

_____

✏ 18. According to Acts:15:5, what one main work of the Old Testament covenant were the Christians of the sect of Pharisees trying to impose upon the Gentile Christians as a condition of salvation?

_____

_____

In Acts 15:9-11, Peter led the council to decide that no works of the Law are required for the salvation of either Jews or Gentiles. Rather, all are saved by faith (verse 9) through grace (verse 11).

✏ 19. Review Acts 15:5,8-11 again, and state in your own words why the New Testament Church took this position.

_____

_____

_____

_____

According to the rest of the New Testament, following this historic meeting, the first century Church continued to teach the doctrine that salvation is only through God's grace by faith in Jesus Christ. Above we have studied only a few of the New Testament Scriptures that show this.

Unfortunately, following the first century, the Church gradually moved away from this pure teaching and progressively added a "works-righteousness" doctrine. The Church began to teach that in order to be truly saved, the believer must do certain other things besides simply accepting Jesus Christ by faith and receiving God's free grace. During the Medieval Period (A.D. 400-1500), most of Christendom taught that believers must be baptized by Church officials and regularly receive the Communion elements administered by the Church. Those who did not were considered unredeemed and damned.

✎ 20. Review Ephesians 2:8,9. In your own words, explain why the teaching that a believer must also participate in activities such as water baptism and Communion to be truly saved is wrong, according to Scripture.

_____

_____

_____

_____

_____

Near the end of the 15th century, more and more thoughtful Christians who studied the Bible begin to realize that this "works-righteousness" requirement for salvation had been added on by the Church. They begin to realize that this doctrine simply was not correct according to Scripture.

Then, during the early years of the 16th century, there were more protests against several doctrines and practices in the Church's traditions at that time. This resulted in a wide-ranging religious renewal movement known as the "Protestant Reformation." Martin Luther, who was a Roman Catholic priest, is usually acknowledged as the first great leader of the Reformation. In protest against the Roman Catholic Church, Luther promoted several doctrines for which the Reformation is now noted. These included the authority of Scripture, which we noted in study 1, and the doctrine of justification by faith, which we are now studying.

Post-Reformation To Present

Because of Reformation leaders such as Martin Luther (1483-1546), John Calvin (1509-1564), and Ulrich Zwingli (1484-1531), the truth that one is saved by grace through faith became an established doctrine and practice for many years. However, as noted in study 1, the Enlightenment Age (18th century) was characterized by extreme rationalism and agnosticism. During this time, the authority of Scripture was challenged and often rejected. And once again, the doctrine of justification by faith in Jesus Christ was threatened.

✎ **21. Read Colossians 2:8. After reviewing this verse, state how Paul's warning speaks to these Enlightenment developments.**

_____

_____

_____

_____

_____

_____

Fortunately, as we learned in the previous study, by the end of the 19th century, spiritual renewal movements such as the Second Great Awakening and the Holiness Movement had begun to recapture the biblical principles of the Reformation. Participants in these movements, who insisted upon the inspiration and authority of the Bible, held strongly to what the Bible says about how individuals are saved. (See Romans 1:16,17, and Ephesians 2:8,9.)

It is especially important to note that, at the beginning of the 20th century, the Pentecostal Movement historically flowed out of the Holiness Movement. Pentecostals held strongly to the principle of justification by faith that came to them from the Reformation and Holiness traditions.

These early Pentecostals also realized the importance of following through with a life of righteousness and true holiness. On the one hand, they agreed with Paul: salvation is by grace through faith in Jesus Christ (Ephesians 2:8,9). On the other hand, they also agreed with James: such salvation will be shown by good works (James 2:18). These early Pentecostals realized that Paul and James were in agreement in their teaching on this point.

SUMMARY

Contemporary Pentecostals hold strongly to the position that salvation is by grace through faith and not by works. No particular work is required for obtaining salvation—only faith in Jesus Christ. This doctrine is primary in Pentecostal heritage because Pentecostals consider salvation by faith to be the beginning of the believer's personal relationship with Jesus Christ. Pentecostals believe that Scripture teaches this position. They, like other Christians, are indebted to the Reformation for rediscovering and redeveloping this most basic truth.

As important as this truth is however, Pentecostals believe that righteous deeds are also directly related to salvation. Salvation by faith is the beginning; but it is only the beginning. As both Paul and James taught, the kind of faith resulting in initial salvation apart from works will produce righteous works in those who believe.

LET'S REVIEW

1. What Scripture passages confirm the idea of justification or salvation by faith and not by works?

_____

_____

2. During the Medieval Period (A.D. 400-1400) the Church commonly taught and practiced a "works-righteousness" doctrine of salvation—believers had to "do" certain things to be saved. What two activities administered by the Church were among the most common of these activities?

_____

_____

3. Name the reform movement of the 16th century that challenged the Medieval Roman Catholic "works-righteousness" doctrine of salvation.

_____

4. Christians of a certain sect were wanting to require one primary "work" of Gentile converts. Identify the sect of Jews and that "work" from Acts 2:5.

_____

_____

5. List the two spiritual renewal movements that helped to restore the justification or salvation by faith doctrine during the 19th century.

_____

_____

6. What passage in James is sometimes thought to contradict Paul's teaching on justification by faith alone? What two passages in Paul's writings show that Paul and James agreed about the relationship of works to saving faith?

_____

_____

_____

STUDY 3

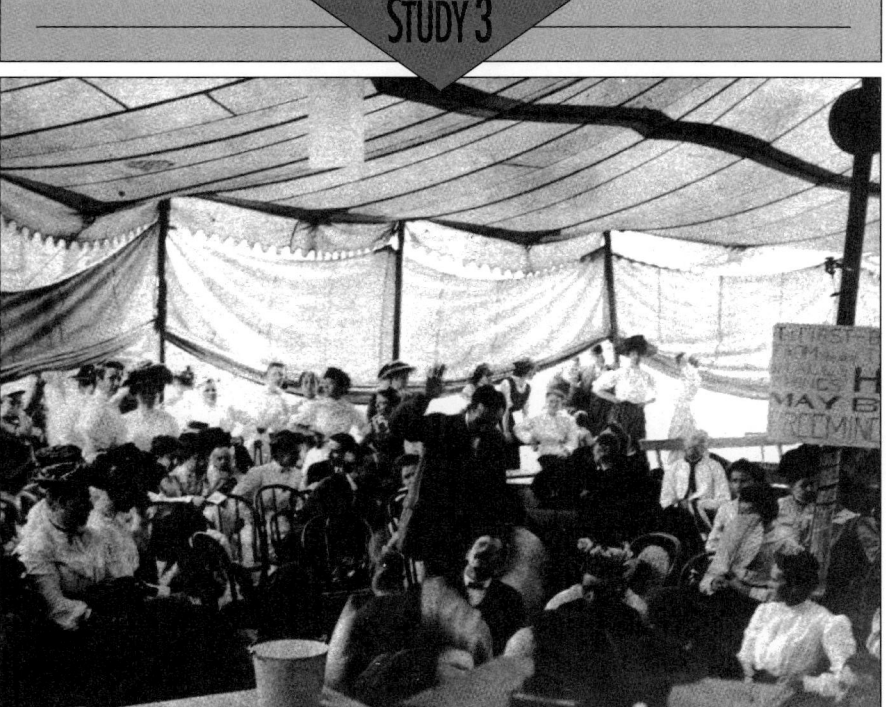

REVIVALISM: REVITALIZED NEW TESTAMENT CHRISTIANITY

In the first study we learned how early in the 20th century when the Pentecostal Movement began, Pentecostals ardently embraced the Reformation principle that Scripture is the final authority for Christian doctrine and practice. Of course, for these early Pentecostals, this meant Scripture was the standard and pattern by which individual Christians are to live and develop their daily lives. But it meant more: The New Testament is to be the pattern or model for the whole Church in every culture and in every age.

These early Pentecostals believed that following the first century, and especially during the Middle Ages, the Church progressively deviated seriously from this New Testament pattern. They recognized the significant, positive developments of renewal provided by the Reformation; they also believed there remained a need for further restoration of the New Testament model. They believed the Book of Acts especially provided the model for the Church in every generation. They also believed revival was needed to restore the contemporary Church to the New Testament pattern pictured in the Book of Acts.

A View From First Corinthians

Read 1 Corinthians 10:11. Note that Paul is telling the Corinthian believers that biblical accounts of things that happened to God's people in the past are examples for them.

Now read 1 Corinthians 10:1-5 and answer the following questions:

1. Who was the leader of God's people at this time?

_____

2. According to verse 5, where were God's people at this time?

_____

Think about how and why these people are examples for believers in later times.

3. State their examples in "negative" terms or what they did that they should not have done.

_____

_____

4. Now, state their examples in "positive" terms or what they should have done.

_____

_____

5. In the light of the last part of verse 11, would you agree that these situations written about in the Bible are also examples for us and all other Christians of all places and all times? Give reasons for your answer.

_____

_____

_____

The Book Of Acts

Pentecostals, and indeed many Evangelicals, believe that the happenings in the Book of Acts are examples for Christians in a way similar to what Paul said in 1 Corinthians with regard to Old Testaments events. What the apostles and believers taught and practiced as recorded in Acts is what Christians should teach and practice in all generations of the Church.

To begin this discussion we need to note the relationship between the Book of Acts and the third Gospel—the Gospel of Luke. The very first verse of Acts links Acts to the Gospel of Luke. In that verse the writer refers to "the former treatise" (KJV), or "my former book" (NIV). In Luke 1:3, Luke addresses his Gospel account to one named "Theophilus." Likewise, the author of Acts addresses this book to one named "Theophilus."

Evangelicals hold to the long-standing Church tradition that says Luke is the author of Acts as correct. Luke, then, is the author of both of these works; the Gospel of Luke being the "former book" referred to in Acts 1:1. Thus, these two books are two volumes in one set.

Further, in Luke 1:1-4, this author indicates why he is writing the material in these two volumes. It is so Theophilus (and all others who read this) "may know the certainty of the things...taught" (NIV). Christians have long understood that the Gospel of Luke, along with the other Gospel accounts, provides the correct fundamental teachings of Christianity that are standard for all generations of the Church. The Book of Acts is the same kind of material. It, too, provides a standard or model for the Church in all generations.

According to the picture provided in the Book of Acts, what then, is the Church to be like? Let's take a look at some verses from Acts to find out.

6. In Acts 1:4,5 what did Jesus, the Head of the Church, command His followers to experience?

_____

7. According to Acts 2:39, is the promise of the Father (Acts 1:4) and the experience of the Day of Pentecost (Acts 2:1-4) only for the first generation of the Church? Give your answer and then write out Acts 2:39.

_____

_____

8. From Acts 2:39, identify the three groups that Peter specifically said this promise is for.

1) _____

2) _____

3) _____

Every generation of the Church should receive the promise of the Father and be Spirit-filled. This can only happen if the individual believers who make up the Church are baptized in the Holy Spirit. This is the pattern established in the first two chapters of Acts; and there is no place in Acts, or elsewhere in the New Testament, where this pattern is changed.

9. Carefully study Acts 8:14-17 and Acts 19:1-6. According to these examples, what should Church leaders do when the Holy Spirit has not yet come upon believers?

_____

_____

Every generation of the Church should witness healings and other signs and wonders with the Holy Spirit working in and through believers.

10. According to Acts 14:3 and 19:11,12, was the performing of signs and wonders a significant characteristic of the Church in Acts? What specifically happened through Paul in Acts 19:12?

_____

_____

Apparently, Luke tells about only a sample of the healings and other miracles that occurred at the hands of the apostles and other believers during the times of Acts.

11. Look at each of the following references and briefly identify the sign or wonder that occurred in each.

Acts 3:1-10 _____

Acts 9:32-35 _____

Acts 9:36-41 _____

Acts 13:6-11 _____

Acts 16:16-18 _____

Acts 16:25,26 _____

During the first century, everyone in the Church should have had the manifestation of the gifts of the Spirit to help it do the work of the Kingdom. Various kinds of gifts, given and manifested by the Spirit, are spoken of in the Epistles as well as in the Book of Acts. Before moving on, turn to 1 Corinthians 12:4-11,28, and Romans 12:6-8 to read Paul's listing of some of the gifts of the Spirit.

Now read Acts 2:14. When Peter "raised his voice" (NIV) on the Day of Pentecost, he was obviously not simply delivering a sermon he had prepared in advance. Rather he was speaking forth under special divine unction of the Holy Spirit.

12. Look again at 1 Corinthians 12:4-11, and identify which one of the gifts of the Spirit was being manifested through Peter on this occasion.

_____

_____

✎ 13. Read Acts 3:1-8. Which gifts listed in 1 Corinthians 12:6-11 were being manifested through Peter in Acts 3:1-8?

_____

_____

✎ 14. According to Acts 6:10, what gift was being manifested through Stephen when he reasoned with the Jews in the Synagogue in Jerusalem?

_____

Finally, in every generation, the Church should be a witnessing outreach. In the very first chapter of Acts, Luke says Jesus told His followers to be baptized in the Holy Spirit in order to be witnesses in their immediate area as well as throughout the earth.

✎ 15. What does Acts 5:28 say about the disciples' witnessing efforts?

_____

_____

✎ 16. In Acts 8:4-8, where did Jesus' followers go witnessing and what were the results?

_____

_____

✎ 17. In Acts 10:1 through 11:18, what specific people groups did Peter witness to concerning salvation through Jesus Christ?

_____

✎ 18. In Acts 11:19-26, Luke tells about believers going to Antioch of Syria and witnessing. As a result a great church developed there. According to verse 20, what specific group of people was witnessed to beside the Jews identified in verse 19?

_____

In Acts 13:1 through 21:16, Luke tells of the witnessing outreach of the Church in four missionary journeys. The first one, with Barnabas and Saul (later called Paul), is recorded in Acts 13 and 14. The account of two more journeys began in Acts 15:36-41. Here Barnabas took Mark and went in one direction, while Paul took Silas and went in another direction. Paul's third missionary journey is recorded in Acts 18:23 through 21:16.

✎ 19. Many Bibles have maps in the back that show the areas these missionary outreaches covered. Look at these maps, and note all of the places Barnabas, Paul, and others went for the specific purpose of witnessing to others about salvation through Jesus Christ.

_____

_____

_____

REFORMATION AND GREAT AWAKENINGS

A study of the Book of Acts reveals that the Church of the first century (the New Testament Church) had certain defining characteristics. For obvious historical reasons, the nature of the Church changed significantly following the first century. Unfortunately, during the Middle Ages, this process continued and became so drastic that by the 15th century, the Church was no longer characterized by the essential elements that defined the first century New Testament Church.

The 16th century Protestant Reformation, led by Martin Luther and other Reformers, did much to restore basic biblical doctrines. However, it would take "revivalism" of later centuries to move forward the process of restoring the Church to its New Testament form.

✎ 20. Look up the word *revivalism* in a dictionary and select the best definition you can find that correlates with our study.

_____

_____

The First Great Awakening during the first half of the 18th century and the Second Great Awakening at the beginning of the 19th century heightened the awareness of this need for restoration. These spiritual awakenings established revivalism as the method of this continuing restoration process. Diverse evangelists like George Whitefield, John Wesley, Jonathan Edwards, Timothy Dwight, and Charles Finney moved a major segment of the Church into revivalism. These ministers and others were responding to the felt need to restore New Testament type faith and practice to Christianity. They preached the need for repentance, born-again salvation experience, and personal relationship with Jesus Christ.

✎ 21. Look up the word *restoration* in a dictionary and select the best definition you can find that correlates with our study.

_____

_____

PENTECOSTAL REVIVAL

At the end of the 19th century, there remained the need for further restoration of the Church to its New Testament form. As noted above, the 16th century Protestant Reformation did much to restore basic biblical doctrines, while the Great Awakenings of the 18th and 19th centuries had restored the concept of a personal salvation experience with God. But many of the inherent characteristics of the New Testament Church, as seen in our study of Acts, were still not a part of the contemporary Church. More specifically, there remained the need to restore the full dynamics of the workings of the Holy Spirit within the Church.

At the turn of the 20th century, some in the revivalism movement began to experience more of the Spirit's dynamics like those seen in Acts. They spoke in tongues, witnessed healings, and experienced other miracles and manifestations of the Spirit.

A minister by the name of Charles F. Parham was one of the leaders of those who experienced these spiritual phenomena. In October 1900, Parham established a Bible school in Topeka, Kansas. One assignment Parham gave his students was to study the Book of Acts to see if believers in New Testament times knew when they had been baptized in the Holy Spirit. Parham's students concluded, "yes," New Testament believers did know when they were baptized in the Holy Spirit because it was accompanied with speaking in tongues (William W. Menzies, *Anointed to Serve*, 36).

On January 1, 1901, one of Parham's students, Agnes Ozman, asked Parham to lay hands on her and pray for her to receive the baptism in the Holy Spirit like they did throughout Acts. When he did, she began to speak in tongues just like the occasions in the Book of Acts. (We will examine these occasions in more detail in a later lesson.) Over the next few weeks, Parham and most of his other students also received the Baptism experience. Of particular significance is the fact that Parham, his students, and others who followed, associated speaking in tongues with the baptism in the Holy Spirit. Thus, this incident is often considered to be the beginning of the 20th century Pentecostal Movement (Menzies 37,38).

There were several other similar occurrences in various places. The next main epicenter of the revival, however, was in Los Angeles, California, at a mission on Azusa Street. The pastor of this mission was William J. Seymour who had learned of the tongues experience earlier under Parham's ministry in Houston, Texas. From the Azusa Street Mission the Pentecostal revival spread across the United States and eventually around the world (Menzies 49-57).

Those who had these kinds of Spiritual experiences were called "Pentecostals" because they believed they had the same experience as the 120 followers of Jesus on the Day of Pentecost as recorded in Acts 2.

SUMMARY

Pentecostals believe that God intends for the Church to always be characterized by the same essential attributes as those exhibited in the Book of Acts. Believers in every generation are to be filled with the Holy Spirit like the first century Christians were. When this is the case, the dynamic presence and power of the Holy Spirit is manifested in and through the body of believers. Signs and wonders, such as healings and other miracles, are common. The Holy Spirit also manifests the spiritual gifts through believers for the purpose of enabling them to effectively build and edify the body of Christ.

LET'S REVIEW

1. What Scriptures indicate that biblical accounts of things which happened to God's people in past times are examples for later believers?

_____

2. In your own words, restate why many evangelicals, including Pentecostals, believe the Book of Acts provides a model for how the Church should be in all generations.

_____

_____

3. From the Book of Acts, list some of the defining aspects of the New Testament Church that are to characterize the Church of today. List at least four or five of the most prominent aspects or characteristics.

_____

_____

_____

_____

4. Identify some of the evangelists who helped restore New Testament type vitality to the Church during the First and Second Great Awakenings.

_____

_____

5. We studied about a special spiritual "revival" or "movement" that began at the turn of the 20th century, restoring the dynamics of the Spirit's ministry within a major segment of the Church. Identify this spiritual revival or movement.

_____

6. Events at a Bible school in Topeka, Kansas, on January 1, 1901, and following are often considered to be the beginning of this special revival movement. Identify the minister who operated this Bible school and became one of the first leaders of this movement.

_____

REVIVALISM: PERSONAL RELATIONSHIP WITH GOD

In this lesson, we are going to study the Pentecostal belief that believers can enter into and constantly experience a personal relationship with God. This is closely related to our second study in which we learned that salvation is a free gift of God's grace and is received by faith. In study 4, we will see that the results of a positive response to God's grace by faith are more than just being judged not guilty by God—the results also include an ongoing relationship with Jesus Christ.

The 16th century Protestant Reformation, led by Martin Luther and other Reformers, especially restored the doctrine of salvation by grace through faith. The reality of a personal relationship with God through Jesus Christ was also restored by the spiritual awakenings studied in chapter 3. These were the First Great Awakening during the first half of the 18th century and the Second Great Awakening during the first half of the 19th century. Later, in the 20th century, the Pentecostal Movement—in the revivalism tradition of these Great Awakenings—gave renewed vitality to the experience of an ongoing, personal relationship with God.

GOD WITH US

God is not just some *force* or *power* or some other kind of impersonal entity out there in the universe or beyond. Rather, He is a personal being who desires to have relationship and fellowship with humanity, which He created.

Significance Of The Incarnation

Read Matthew 1:18-23. God's desire to have relationship and fellowship with mankind is in fact the wonderful truth of the *Incarnation*. This is the reason why we are now considering this passage in Matthew. As you will notice, this passage is part of Matthew's account of Jesus' birth.

1. Look up the term *Incarnation* in a dictionary and write the definition that best fits our study.

_____

_____

2. Look at Matthew 1:18-23 again. What was the name given to Mary's son (that is, God's Son) according to verse 21? What was the particular meaning and significance of this name?

_____

_____

3. Jesus is certainly the most common name that Christians use to refer to God's Son; but He is identified by another name. According to Matthew 1:23, what is the other special name by which Jesus is to be identified? What is the particular meaning and significance of this name?

_____

_____

Importance Of Relationship

God does not desire to be separated from us and unrelated to us. Rather, the Scriptures clearly reveal He desires to be with us in personal relationship. The following passages that we will consider highlight some of the particulars of that relationship with God.

Children Of God

Read John 1:12 and Galatians 3:26. The first Scripture verse was written by the apostle John, one of Jesus' first followers. The second was written by the apostle Paul in the middle of his teaching about salvation by faith. The primary topic in both is salvation or redemption, but also note the emphasis on *relationship*.

✏️ **4.** In John 1:12 and Galatians 3:26, John and Paul used similar terms to emphasize relationship. Look at both of these verses again and identify the special term of relationship. Write it in the blank below.

_____

_____

John said that this relationship of being God's "children" is the "right" or "privilege" of those who receive Jesus. Paul stated that we are "sons of God" through "faith" in Jesus Christ. Salvation includes the privilege of child-to-father relationship with God himself.

Read Romans 8:14-16. This is another passage that highlights the believer's personal relationship with God. As you read this passage, notice that Paul again speaks of the believer's relationship to God using the same terms—"sons" or "children"—that we saw in John 1:12 and Galatians 3:26.

✏️ **5.** In Romans 8:15, what was the special phrase that Paul used to speak of how believers become sons of God? This term is used to emphasize that God made a _deliberate_ choice to bring us into a family relationship with Him.

_____

_____

✏️ **6.** With this great truth in mind, look again especially at Romans 8:16. In one to three sentences tell of the personal importance this verse brings to you.

_____

_____

_____

Christians who believe in a "born-again" experience and enter into a personal relationship with God, commonly hold to what is sometimes called "know-so" salvation. That is, according to Romans 8:16, a believer can know that he or she is in proper relationship with God because God's own Spirit witnesses this reality to the child of God.

✏️ **7.** In Romans 8:16, Paul said: "The Spirit himself bears witness with our spirit that we are children of God." Describe what you believe Paul meant by "bears witness with."

_____

_____

Eternal Life

John 17:3 is part of a prayer Jesus prayed for those who would believe on Him. In the first phrase of this verse, "eternal life" is identified as one of the aspects of salvation.

✎8. In the second phrase of John 17:3, what is "eternal life" equated with?

_____

In this passage, the term "know" means much more than to simply "know about." Rather, it means to know by experience. In fact, it is not inappropriate to substitute the term "experience" for the term "know" in this verse. Try reading it that way and notice the impact!

Fellowship

Read 1 John 1:3. The apostle John is also the author of this verse. Writing out of his own experience, he shares another very important aspect of the believer's relationship with God.

✎9. In 1 John 1:3, identify the key term that speaks of Christians' relationships to each other, to the Heavenly Father, and to Jesus Christ.

_____

_____

In using the term, "fellowship," the apostle John assured us that our relationship with the Almighty, Holy God is much more than some nebulous connection to an impersonal *force* or *power*.

Identification With Believers

Finally in this section, we are considering an incident recorded in the Book of Acts that emphasizes the personal relationship of God to His children. This incident, which is recorded three times in the Book of Acts, lets us know how closely Jesus identifies himself with believers.

Read Acts 9:4; 22:7; and 26:14. The occasion was very early in the Church when Saul was leading an organized persecution of Christians following the stoning of Stephen (Acts 7:54 through 8:3). Saul had obtained official papers from the Jewish religious leaders in Jerusalem to go to synagogues far and wide to find the followers of Jesus and bring them back to Jerusalem (Acts 9:1-2). One day, on his way to Damascus for just such a purpose, Saul was knocked to the ground by a bright light out of heaven, and he heard the voice of the risen, ascended Lord Jesus Christ. Saul was rebuked by the Lord for his activity of persecuting Christians.

✎10. Read Acts 9:4; 22:7; 26:14 again and carefully note whom Jesus specifically said Saul was persecuting.

Circle one: A) Christians   B) Believers   C) "Me"— Jesus

✎11. What does this tell us about God's personal identification with us as His children?

_____

As children of God, we are Jesus' brothers and sisters. He considers us to be one with Him. As far as He is concerned, what happens to us happens to Him.

HISTORICAL PERSPECTIVE

Views Of God In The Middle Ages

Our study shows that the apostles and other early Christians understood their relationship with God to be very intimate and personal. To them, God was their Father and He identified with them through His Son Jesus Christ. This conception of the believer's relationship with God was reasonably maintained for a few centuries. During those early centuries, those who considered themselves to be "Christians" usually understood and experienced personal relationship with God through Jesus Christ.

However, because of ignorance and the impersonal ritualism of the Church, by the Middle Ages (A.D. 500-1500), many who considered themselves to be "Christians" never experienced a personal relationship with God. For them, contact with God all too often was limited to their participation in sacraments administered by the Church. Of course, some did experience the reality of personal relationship with God; but generally, relating to God was understood to be only through some other human intermediary such as a priest.

Unfortunately, this condition continued for many years until the 16th century. As we discussed in study 2 and study 3, the Protestant Reformation began to restore some basic scriptural doctrines.

✎ 12. Briefly review study 2 and identify the specific Reformation doctrine that is directly related to this lesson. Write it on the lines below.

_____

_____

_____

Age Of Enlightenment

The reality of a personal relationship with God was once again damaged by various teachings coming out of the 18th century Age of Enlightenment. The rationalism and extremes of scientific objectivity during this period did not allow for the subjective notion of a mystical, personal relationship with a divine being.

During the Age of Enlightenment, many unusual views of God emerged. One that especially exemplified this age was *deism*. Deism pictured God as being remote and uninvolved with His creation.

✎ 13. Look up the term *deism* in an encyclopedia and list some of the things you find.

_____

_____

Second Great Awakening

During the first half of the 19th century, the Second Great Awakening reestablished the biblical concepts of repentance, born-again salvation experience, and personal relationship with Jesus Christ. The beginning of this spiritual awakening is usually dated near the end of the 18th century under the leadership of Timothy Dwight, then president of Yale University. However, the revivalism methods that especially characterized this awakening were mostly developed following 1824 by evangelist Charles Finney.

Finney and others who followed his revivalism methods directed their salvation messages toward the individual. They expected seekers to experience a conversion that was followed by an ongoing personal relationship with God. Finney is especially noted for developing and establishing the forms and methods of contemporary revivalism. Many other evangelists such as Asa Mahan, Dwight L. Moody, and Billy Graham continued this focus through the remainder of the 19th century and on into the 20th century. The reality of individual salvation and personal relationship with God was finally reestablished in the Church.

Holiness And Pentecostal Movements

At the turn of the 20th century, the Holiness Movement and the Pentecostal Movement flowed out of the Second Great Awakening. Both of these movements continued to emphasize the reality of individual spiritual experiences and personal relationship with God through Jesus Christ.

Besides an initial born-again salvation experience, the Holiness Movement also taught the idea of a subsequent, crisis experience of entire sanctification. In Holiness Movement understanding, this crisis sanctification experience was then followed by continuing, progressive sanctification. We will study this doctrine more fully in our next lesson.

Likewise, the Pentecostal Movement, which began at the turn of the 20th century, also insisted upon the reality of personal experience and relationship with God. Besides born-again salvation, Pentecostals also taught and experienced the baptism in the Holy Spirit with speaking in tongues and daily fellowship with God by walking in the Spirit. (This will be examined in a later study.) The Second Great Awakening of early 19th century reestablished the experience of personal relationship with God; and this reality has been and continues to be a vital aspect of Pentecostal teaching and experience.

SUMMARY

Pentecostals hold that God desires to have a personal relationship with believers. He has made this possible through His Son Jesus Christ. *Salvation* not only means that the believer is forgiven of past sins, but he or she is also privileged to be a "child of God." Because of this wonderful relationship, the believer has ongoing fellowship with the loving Heavenly Father. This fellowship is a work of the Holy Spirit who communes with the spirit of the believer so each believer can know he or she is a child of God.

LET'S REVIEW

1. In Matthew 1:21, the angel told Joseph to give a specific name to the Son of God. What is that name and what is its significance?

_____

_____

_____

2. According to Matthew 1:23, what is the wonderful meaning of the name "Immanuel" that was applied to Jesus at His birth? How does this name make Jesus more personal?

_____

_____

3. Identify the family relationship that believers are privileged to have with God according to John 1:12; Galatians 3:26; and Romans 8:14-16.

_____

_____

4. What significant term did John use in 1 John 1:3 to describe the believer's relationship with God the Father and His Son Jesus Christ?

_____

5. Identify the theological belief system of the 18th century that pictured God as being remote and uninvolved with His creation.

_____

_____

_____

6. The Second Great Awakening is usually considered to have begun late in the 18th century under the leadership of Timothy Dwight. But the major part of this awakening was during the first half of the 19th century. Identify the evangelist who established revivalism during this time.

_____

HOLINESS MOVEMENT: SANCTIFICATION

The Holiness Movement began in the 19th century and continued into the 20th century. Several times in previous lessons we have briefly noted that historically the contemporary Pentecostal Movement flowed out of the Holiness Movement. In fact, most of those who first experienced speaking in tongues at the turn of the 20th century were associated with the Holiness Movement.

In this lesson, our special focus will be the doctrine of sanctification. We will also study the historical details of how the Pentecostal Movement is related to the Holiness Movement. As the term *holiness* indicates, emphasis upon the doctrine of sanctification was a hallmark of the Holiness Movement. This doctrine also became a characteristic feature of the Pentecostal Movement.

SANCTIFICATION AND HOLINESS

The terms *sanctification* and *holiness* are synonymous terms. Sanctification means the state of being set apart to a sacred purpose or to a religious use. It also means the state of being free from sin. Holiness means the quality or state of being sacred and pure or set apart to the service of God.

From these definitions we note that the most basic, fundamental thrust of sanctification and holiness is the idea of being *prepared*, *set apart*, and *used for a special purpose*. In the Old Testament, the holy vessels in the tabernacle and the temple were made of the same kind of gold and silver as other vessels among the people. Nevertheless, the vessels in the tabernacle and temple were considered to be sanctified because they were *prepared*, *set apart*, and *used for a special purpose*.

Likewise, in the Old Testament, God's chosen people, Israel, were considered by God to be holy or sanctified even though they were often disobedient and faithless. They were saints, not because they were fundamentally better than other people, but because God wanted to prepare them as a selected group for His special purpose of bringing His plan of redemption to all of mankind.

Observe that the idea of holiness or sanctification can be applied to both material things and human beings. When it is applied to material things, the process is rather mechanical and arbitrary. Also, since material things do not have a will, the process of sanctifying them is totally aside from any cooperation on the part of that which is sanctified. For example, in the case of the holy vessels in the Old Testament, God arbitrarily selected some gold and silver vessels from among others to be placed in the tabernacle and temple for use there. However, in the case of people, the factor of the human will makes the process of sanctification a much more dynamic matter.

There is a considerable amount of Scripture that helps us understand the idea of holiness and its essential importance in the true Christian experience. We will especially want to understand the dynamics of sanctification in the believer, who must exercise his or her will to cooperate with the Holy Spirit in the process. When studying the idea of the believer's sanctification in Scripture, we commonly identify two aspects in the process. These are often termed *Initial Sanctification* and *Continuing Sanctification*.

SANCTIFICATION: INITIAL OR CONTINUAL?

✎1. When Paul wrote to the believers at Corinth in 1 Corinthians 1:2, he stated that they were "called to be saints" (KJV), not by their will or actions. In this verse, how did Paul say that these believers are sanctified?

_____

_____

Everyone who believes in the Lord Jesus Christ and accepts Him as Savior is sanctified in Christ Jesus because Christ Jesus is sanctified; and all who are *in* Him are sanctified simply because they are *in* Him. This is the "initial" aspect of sanctification. The moment the individual believes, he or she is placed in the body of Christ and is sanctified *in* Him. This aspect of sanctification is called *Positional*

Sanctification because it is based solely upon one's "position" in Christ. It is also called *Instantaneous Sanctification* because it begins the moment the believer accepts Jesus as Savior and Sanctifier.

Being positioned in the body of Christ and, therefore, sanctified, is a good beginning; however, it is only a beginning. God intends to continue the process of sanctification in a believer so long as the believer responds in trust in and obedience to God. The sanctification process that follows the born-again, salvation experience is often termed *Continuing Sanctification*.

2. In 2 Corinthians 3:18, Paul used some interesting imagery to discuss the continuing aspect of sanctification. What did Paul say the believer's face was a reflection of?

_____

3. According to 2 Corinthians 3:18, what happens to the believer when he or she continues to behold the glory of the Lord?

_____

_____

_____

According to 2 Corinthians 3:18, this aspect of sanctification is step-by-step; or in Paul's word, it is "from glory to glory." In this verse we see that the continuing aspect of sanctification is *progressive*. As the believer continues to yield to the Holy Spirit, he or she is gradually transformed more and more into the image of Jesus Christ.

This second aspect of sanctification is also called *Actual Sanctification*, because in this process the believer's character actually becomes more and more like the character of Jesus Christ. Here, the sanctification that began by the believer's being positioned in Christ becomes real—actual holiness of character like the character of Jesus Christ.

The whole New Testament teaches that sanctification is a work of the Spirit, as Paul plainly stated in 2 Thessalonians 2:13. This is part of the reason He is called the "Holy" Spirit. But sanctification is also contingent upon the responsive cooperation and faithful activity of the individual as the Holy Spirit seeks to do His work.

4. In 2 Timothy 2:21, Paul said that a man (or woman): (Circle the appropriate letter to complete the statement.)

A. is cleansed by the Word.
B. is cleansed by the Holy Spirit.
C. cleanses himself (or herself).

Does this mean that an individual can cleanse himself or herself and thereby become a sanctified vessel of honor all by his or her own work alone? No, but it certainly does mean that the individual must be a genuine, active participant in the process.

✎ 5. Read 2 Corinthians 7:1 and focus on the middle part of the verse. Here Paul specifically indicated that the "perfecting of holiness in the fear of God" is accomplished when: (Circle the letter of the correct response.)

A. the Holy Spirit cleanses the believer from all defilement of flesh and spirit.
B. we believers cleanse ourselves from all defilement of flesh and spirit.

Again, this verse does not teach that the Holy Spirit does not do the work of sanctification within the believer—His sanctifying power is, of course, absolutely necessary. Without His miraculous work, holiness would not be accomplished in any human being. But this verse also teaches that the Holy Spirit can accomplish sanctification within the believer *only* if the believer works with the Holy Spirit and exercises his or her will positively towards God.

The gold and silver material used to make the vessels for the tabernacle and temple had no will of its own. And its quality and character was not any better than other similar gold and silver. Therefore, those vessels were "holy" only because they were set aside for use in the tabernacle or temple. But obviously, this is not the case with human beings. God graciously offers His plan of redemption and makes the power of the Holy Spirit available. God does not force himself upon a person; but if an individual responds positively, the Holy Spirit begins the work of sanctification. If the believer continues to cooperate willingly, the Holy Spirit continues to do the work of sanctification in his or her life. That believer, then, progressively develops characteristics like those of Jesus Christ.

Unfortunately, some people seem to have some rather negative ideas concerning holiness. They think of it as being only outward legalism. They may believe that no one can really be holy in the true sense. But we have already seen that such views are not the teaching of Scripture. True holiness is not legalistic. Rather, it begins by the power of the Holy Spirit on the inside and progressively develops outwardly into a natural display of Christlike character. And the Bible teaches that God expects believers to continually display this Christlike holiness. He expects this because it is His will and He knows that with the assistance of the Holy Spirit it is possible.

✎ 6. Read 1 Peter 1:13-16 and select the statement below that best agrees with the teaching in this passage:

A. Holiness is a *option* that God makes available to believers.
B. God *expects* all of His obedient children to be holy.

✎ 7. According to 2 Corinthians 7:1, did Paul think that Christians can really be cleansed from all defilement of the flesh and spirit? What was Paul's view on living a truly perfect and holy life?

_____

_____

_____

✎ **8. Read 2 Corinthians 6:18 through 7:1. What is the promise upon which Paul based his conviction that Christians can be cleansed from all defilement and can perfect holiness in their lives?**

_____

_____

God expects His children to be holy simply because that is His character. But there is another reason why God wants believers to be holy. Being holy or sanctified prepares Christians for a special purpose.

✎ **9. Read 2 Timothy 2:20,21 to discover the special purpose that God has in mind for holy individuals. Write it below in your own words.**

_____

_____

_____

_____

First Century To The 18th Century

Earlier in this lesson we observed that the purpose of service is closely connected to the idea of sanctification or holiness. We have already noted that both material things and people were prepared and set apart for the purpose of service in Old Testament times. The holy vessels of the tabernacle and temple were sanctified especially because of their special place of service. Likewise, the people of Israel were called saints, not because they were always really holy in character and obedience toward God, but because God had chosen them to serve as instruments for bringing redemption to all of mankind.

✎ **10. Holy living is simply living the way God wants us to live in order to accomplish what God desires. With this in mind, read Romans 12:1,2. Briefly write your thoughts concerning the relationship of sanctification (holy living) to Christian service.**

_____

_____

_____

_____

Our study has shown that sanctification or holiness is the will of God for believers. In fact, there are many other Scripture passages on this topic that we have not used in this study. The Book of Acts and the Epistles show that the first century Christians understood the importance of living their lives in a holy manner. However, as in the case of other doctrines which we have studied in previous lessons, the doctrine and practice of holiness was largely lost during the Middle Ages (A.D. 500-1500).

Other important biblical doctrines began to be restored during the 16th century Protestant Reformation; unfortunately, this doctrine was not a notable part of the Reformation's focus. In fact, it was not significantly emphasized again until the 18th century. John Wesley (1703-1791), one of the leaders of the First Great Awakening, began to emphasize holiness in his life and in his teaching following a personal spiritual experience in 1738.

Wesley was a minister in the Church of England, which was a rather formal church. Even though it was considered to be quite unconventional, Wesley joined George Whitefield and other ministers in conducting outdoor meetings in which they preached the need for repentance, born-again salvation experience, and personal relationship with Jesus Christ. Wesley also traveled by horse through the English countryside where he preached and left behind well-established prayer groups. Wesley's methods and message were often considered to be very radical. Eventually, his followers broke with the Church of England and established the Methodist Church both in England and America.

Prior to his personal spiritual experience in 1738, Wesley had been in contact with the Moravians, a German Protestant group who stressed disciplined Christian living. Because of this Moravian influence and his own personal experience, Wesley came to believe that living a sanctified life was just as important as experiencing initial salvation. He believed that following his special spiritual experience, the Holy Spirit especially helped him to live a holy life. Because of this emphasis and his personal life of holiness, Wesley's name and ministry became especially identified with the doctrine of sanctification.

✎ 11. Do some research on John Wesley to learn more about the impact of his life and ministry. Most standard encyclopedias will have at least a short article on John Wesley. If you find some additional interesting information about Wesley and his teachings on sanctification, make some brief notes here (or on another sheet of paper) for use in class discussion.

_____

_____

_____

19TH CENTURY HOLINESS MOVEMENT

During the latter half of the 18th century, much of the influence of the First Great Awakening was largely dissipated. But by the dawn of the 19th century, yet another spiritual renewal movement was beginning. This renewal movement became know as the Second Great Awakening. Although, in America, it began in small colleges on the East Coast, it was destined to have its greatest impact out in the western frontier forest regions. It was here that the revivalistic forest camp meeting was born.

While these revival camp meetings were first started primarily by Baptist and

Presbyterian ministers, the extent of the Second Great Awakening was most effectively expanded by the newly emerging Methodist movement. In 1800, there were only about 3,000 Methodists in America. But by 1844, the Methodist Church had grown to be the largest denomination in America with over a million members. This was accomplished by the Methodists combining the revivalistic camp meeting technique with their unique "Circuit Riding Preacher" strategy.

During the years of this great renewal movement, many in the rapidly growing Methodist Church began to believe that Wesley's emphasis on sanctification was being neglected. In 1825, Timothy Merritt, a prominent Methodist, published a treatise on "Christian Perfection," stressing the need for entire sanctification. By this time Charles G. Finney had emerged as the leading revivalist in what became known as "The Great Holiness Revival." In 1835, Merritt began publishing a periodical called the *Guide to Christian Perfection*, in which he espoused his understanding of Wesley's doctrine of sanctification. These were the beginnings of what we have previously identified as the "Holiness Movement."

As the Holiness Movement grew there was an increasing focus upon the idea that beside initial salvation, Christians also needed to experience *entire sanctification*. Those leading the Holiness Movement said Wesley believed that beside the first work of grace that occurred at the time of initial salvation, there needed to be a "second definite work of grace" in which the Holy Spirit entirely sanctified the believer. This became known as the "second definite work of grace" doctrine.

Those who espoused this doctrine pointed out that justification is one work of the Holy Spirit; but sanctification is yet another work of the Holy Spirit. In justification, the repentant sinner receives pardon or the forgiveness of personal sins. Also, in justification, the righteousness of Christ is imputed or attributed to the believer. This is the beginning of the work of sanctification. Another work of sanctification, to deal with the sin nature, is yet necessary.

All people have sinful natures because, in some mysterious manner, all people have inherited the results of Adam's original sin. Even though the repentant sinner has forgiveness and Christ's imputed righteousness, the further work of sanctification is also necessary in order to completely eliminate the effects of original sin. According to the Holiness Movement teachers, the Holy Spirit eradicates original sin in the second definite work of grace. Following this, the Holy Spirit continues the work of sanctification, imparting true, personal righteousness in the believer. Eventually, this sanctifying work restores, in the believer, original righteousness like Adam had before the Fall.

12. Look up the word *sin* in a dictionary. If you can locate a theological dictionary, look up the *doctrine of original sin*. On the lines below, write some comments you find interesting on the subject.

_____

_____

_____

Those in the Holiness Movement taught that sanctification is both instantaneous and progressive. It begins instantaneously at the time of initial salvation with the cleansing of personal sins and the imputing of Christ's righteousness. From the time of initial salvation, if the believer continues to respond positively to God, the Holy Spirit continues the work of sanctification. Progressively, the believer is brought to a place of total submission; and, at that point the sin nature is destroyed. This second definite work of grace experience is called "entire sanctification." Following this special second experience, as long as the believer continues to cooperate, the Holy Spirit continues the work of sanctification in which He progressively restores Adam's original righteousness within the believer. Therefore, the sanctified believer can consistently resist temptation and live a holy life of victory over sin.

✎ 13. Do some research on the Holiness Movement and its teaching on sanctification. Look under the headings "Holiness Movement," "Sanctification," and/or "Wesley, John." If you are able to find some interesting information that you think would make a contribution to class discussion, make some brief notes below.

_____

_____

_____

TURN OF THE 20TH CENTURY

During the last quarter of the 19 century, the Holiness Movement continued to grow, becoming a significant, separately identifiable entity within Methodism. It also impacted other major Protestant denominations in America and became truly national in scope. However, because of the "second definite work of grace" doctrine and a strong focus upon outward holiness, the Holiness Movement became increasingly controversial especially within Methodism. Eventually, those who taught this particular doctrine of sanctification were forced to leave the Methodist Church. By the end of the century several small Holiness denominations were formed. There were also numerous Methodist ministers who left their church and became independent Holiness ministers.

In October 1900, one of these independent Holiness ministers, Charles Parham, went to Topeka, Kansas, and started a Bible school for training young people to be ministers. Later that fall, Parham became interested in the biblical idea of the "baptism in the Holy Spirit" and wondered about its relationship to sanctification. Like other Holiness ministers, Parham believed that sanctification was a process that began at initial salvation, but also included a "second definite work of grace" that he called "entire sanctification." Parham believed and taught the doctrine of sanctification as we have described in the paragraph immediately before item 13.

In December of 1900, Parham had revival meetings scheduled in Kansas City. He decided to give his Bible school students an assignment and leave them in Topeka while he went to Kansas City. He told them to study the Book of Acts to discover what it said about the baptism in the Holy Spirit, and be prepared to give him a report when he returned later that month. At the end of December Parham returned to Topeka, gathered his students together, and asked them for their reports. On the basis of their study, Parham's students had decided that the baptism in the Holy Spirit described in Acts was an experience that they should receive. Further, they concluded that Christians today would know when they received this baptism because they would speak in tongues like the believers in the Book of Acts.

✎14. Read Acts 1:1 through 2:47; 8:14-17; 10:1-48. Write down some comments on what you find that might be similar to the research done by Parham's students concerning the baptism in the Holy Spirit. (Use a separate sheet of paper if more space is needed.)

_____

_____

_____

_____

Since it was New Year's Eve, Parham and his students decided to have a "watch night service" to pray in the new year and the new century. Then, sometime on January 1, 1901, one of the students named Agnes Ozman asked Parham to lay hands on her and pray for her to receive the baptism in the Holy Spirit as the believers had in New Testament times. As Parham prayed, Ozman began to speak in tongues as the Spirit gave the utterance. In the next few days, Parham himself and over 30 other students had the same kind of experience, speaking in tongues like the believers in the Book of Acts.

Historical studies reveal that before this Topeka incident other Christians had also experienced speaking in tongues, especially during the last half of the 19th century. However, in these other occasions, those who had the experience apparently did not so clearly associate speaking in tongues with the idea of the baptism in the Holy Spirit. Many historians believe that the Pentecostal revival survived and flourished directly because Parham and his students connected their experience of speaking in tongues with the biblical experience of the baptism in the Holy Spirit. Because of this, the Topeka incident is often considered to be the birth of the present-day Pentecostal Movement.

Following the Topeka incident, Parham and his students went out to various places preaching their new understanding of the baptism in the Holy Spirit. Because of their previous teaching, they believed that the Baptism was a "third definite work of grace" following initial salvation and entire sanctification. As a result of their revival services, numerous Holiness/Pentecostal churches were established in Kansas, Arkansas, Oklahoma, and Texas. In Texas, Parham established another Bible school, and it was there that William J. Seymour heard Parham teaching about the baptism in the Holy Spirit and speaking in tongues. Seymour took the message to Los Angeles and established the Azusa Street Mission. From about 1906 to 1908 that Pentecostal mission was the epicenter from which the Pentecostal Revival swept back across the United States.

Especially during the first decade of the revival, most of those who had this experience of speaking in tongues were associated with various Holiness churches. Entire Holiness denominations such as the Cleveland, Tennessee, based Church of God, the Pentecostal Holiness Church, and the Church of God in Christ were swept into the rapidly expanding Pentecostal Movement. Most all of the thousands of new Pentecostal Christians believed in the doctrine of entire sanctification as a second definite work of grace. In view of their new experience of speaking in tongues, they simply concluded that the baptism in the Holy Spirit was a third definite work of grace.

By 1910, the Pentecostal revival was beginning to reach more and more Christians who were outside of the Holiness Movement ranks. Believers from various other church backgrounds had the experience of speaking in tongues. But these new Pentecostals did not believe that sanctification included a second definite work of grace. Most notable among these was William Durham, a Baptist minister.

Durham attended Seymour's Azusa Street Mission where, like thousands of others, he experienced speaking in tongues. He believed this experience was the baptism in the Holy Spirit. Although Durham was of Baptist background prior to his Pentecostal experience, he had associations with the Holiness Movement. And apparently he had even taught the "second definite work of grace" sanctification doctrine. Following his baptism in the Holy Spirit, he endeavored to fellowship and minister among the Holiness/ Pentecostal groups. However, at the time, Durham changed his position on sanctification and could no longer accept the Holiness Movement's view of a second definite work of grace. Rather, he began to teach that it does not take two works of grace to save and cleanse an individual. Durham believed that the beginning work of sanctification at the time of salvation includes more than just forgiveness and cleansing of personal sin. He held that in initial sanctification the Holy Spirit also deals with the sin nature, purging from the individual the defilement of original sin. Durham agreed that following initial sanctification the Holy Spirit gradually reproduces the image of Christ and personal righteousness with the believer. But he rejected the notion that this includes a second definite work of grace like the Holiness Movement taught.

When Durham began to preach his new view on sanctification among the Holiness/ Pentecostal missions and churches, he was strongly opposed by those who firmly held to the concept of three definite works of grace. But Durham was joined in his position by the ever-increasing number of new Pentecostals who were coming into the revival from church backgrounds other than the Holiness Movement. In a few years there was a large number of Pentecostals who shared Durham's view that the process of sanctification does not include a second definite work of grace. They allowed that there are many times when the Holy Spirit does special works of grace in the life of the believer in the ongoing process of sanctification; but they denied that this included a second definite work.

In 1914, when the Assemblies of God was formed in Hot Springs, Arkansas, this new Pentecostal fellowship embraced a position on sanctification that was similar to Durham's view. They took the position that sanctification begins at the time of initial salvation and includes a complete cleansing from all sin at that time. Believers are enabled to live a life of victory over sin by the power of the Holy Spirit, without the need of a second definite work of grace for sanctification.

Other large Pentecostal/Holiness type churches, such as the Church of God (Cleveland, Tennessee), the International Pentecostal Holiness Church, and the Church of God in Christ, continued to hold to the doctrine that a second definite work of grace is needed for entire sanctification. They would often testify that they had been "saved, sanctified, and filled with the Holy Ghost," signifying that they believed in three definite works of grace.

SUMMARY

Pentecostals believe that a Christian can live a consistent, holy life of victory over sin. In the work of sanctification, the Holy Spirit cleanses the sinner from personal sins and also purges the believer from the defilement of original sin. This sanctifying work is both instantaneous and progressive. At the time of salvation, the Holy Spirit imputes to the believer the righteousness of Christ and the believer is instantly sanctified. Following salvation, as the believer cooperates and works with the Holy Spirit, the Holy Spirit progressively imparts Christlike character, producing the fruit of the Spirit and true righteousness in the believer.

LET'S REVIEW

✏️1. From the definitions given at the beginning of this study, restate the most basic, fundamental thrust of the terms *sanctification* and *holiness.*

_____

_____

✏️2. Identify the two aspects in the process of sanctification and give at least one Scripture reference that speaks of each aspect.

_____

_____

✏️3. Name the minister in the Church of England who, during the first part of 18th century, went through the English countryside emphasizing holiness in his personal life and in his teaching. His name and ministry became especially identified with the doctrine of sanctification.

_____

✏️4. Especially during the last half of the 19th century, the Holiness Movement emphasized Christian perfection and taught that entire sanctification requires a second definite work of grace. Briefly explain why they thought this second work of grace was necessary.

_____

_____

✏️5. During the first quarter of the 19th century, two views concerning the timing of sanctification emerged among Pentecostal believers. Name the two views.

_____

_____

✏️6. Why did William Durham begin to believe and teach that a second definite work of grace for sanctification was incorrect doctrine?

_____

_____

HOLINESS MOVEMENT: BAPTISM IN THE HOLY SPIRIT

ontemporary Pentecostals believe that on the Day of Pentecost, following Jesus' ascension back to heaven, God began pouring out His Spirit
for the purpose of enabling the Church to accomplish a divine task. They
believe that, beginning then, God desired every born-again Christian to be
empowered by the Spirit to do the work of evangelism and discipleship.

Unfortunately, from the second to the 19th century, the Church as a
whole usually did not understand this. Therefore, during those centuries
Christians usually did not experience the dynamic enablement of the Holy
Spirit as they did during the first century.

In this lesson we will study more fully what Pentecostals believe concerning the baptism in the Holy Spirit and the ongoing, dynamic workings
of the Spirit in the Church today. We will also see why Pentecostals believe
that this experience and these manifestations of the Spirit are vitally important to the contemporary Church.

BIBLICAL BASIS

Evidence Of The Baptism In The Holy Spirit

Read Acts 1:4-9. Luke recorded Jesus' last words to His followers before His ascension back to heaven (verse 9). No doubt Jesus felt very strongly about these final instructions to His followers since He was leaving them with a special task.

✏1. Read Acts 1:5. Why did Jesus want His followers to wait in Jerusalem??

_____

✏2. Who did Jesus say promised to baptize the disciples in the Holy Spirit (Acts 1:4)?

_____

✏3. Read Acts 1:8. Why did the Father and Jesus want His followers to experience the baptism in the Holy Spirit, and what was the purpose of the baptism in the Holy Spirit?

_____

_____

_____

Jesus wanted His followers to experience the baptism in the Holy Spirit in order to enable them to accomplish the task He had spoken about earlier. Luke recorded God's plan in the last part of his Gospel account—that the gospel of Jesus Christ be proclaimed to all the nations, beginning from Jerusalem (Luke 24:47). Jesus knew that His followers could not accomplish this task simply in their own power.

So, the purpose of the baptism in the Holy Spirit is to enable believers to be supernaturally effective in world evangelism and discipleship. A couple of questions should be asked. First, "Has the task of world evangelism and discipleship been fully completed yet?" The obvious answer to this question is "No." And second, "Could anyone possibly suppose that Christians today are anymore capable than the apostles of accomplishing that task simply in their own power?" Again, the obvious answer to the question is "No." This is why Pentecostals believe it is still the Father's will for all believers to be baptized in the Holy Spirit and thereby be especially empowered by the Spirit to be witnesses.

A thorough search of the New Testament reveals only five instances in which Scripture writers discussed the specific experience we call the "baptism in the Holy Spirit." Luke recorded all five of these in Acts 2:1-4; 8:4-19; 9:17-19; 10:44-46; 11:16,17; and 19:1-6. In one of these incidents, the case of the apostle Paul (Acts 9:17-19), Luke did not give many details. When Ananias ministered to Paul, at that time called "Saul," he promised Saul that he would regain his sight and become filled with the Holy Spirit. But Luke did not say what happened in regard to Saul's being filled with the Holy Spirit.

However, in the other four incidents, Luke did give considerable details of what happened when believers experienced the baptism in the Holy Spirit. In the following paragraphs we will discuss these four incidents. They are as follows: (1) Day of Pentecost, Acts 2:1-4; (2) believers in Samaria, Acts 8:4-19; (3) the house of Cornelius, Acts 10:44-46 and 11:15-17; and (4) disciples at Ephesus, Acts 19:1-6. The first incident was on the first Day of Pentecost following Jesus' ascension back to heaven. Read about this in Acts 2:1-4.

✎4. What were the three supernatural signs that occurred on the Day of Pentecost?

_____

_____

_____

✎5. According to Acts 2:4, specifically which one of these supernatural signs occurred when they were filled with the Holy Spirit?

_____

_____

Before moving to the second incident, observe that "filled with the Holy Spirit" in Acts 2:4 is obviously the fulfillment of Jesus' promise that they would be "baptized in the Holy Spirit" in Acts 1:5.

Now, carefully study the second incident, the believers at Samaria, in Acts 8:4-19. Note that according to verse 12, these Samaritans were full converts to Jesus Christ—what we would term "born-again" believers. They were also baptized in water.

✎6. According to Acts 8:14, who was dispatched from Jerusalem to Samaria?

_____

_____

Notice that according to Acts 8:15,16, the reason Peter and John were dispatched to Samaria was the Samaritan believers had not yet received the Holy Spirit (verse 15), that is "He had not yet fallen upon any of them" (NASB, verse 16).

Does this mean that they did not have the Spirit dwelling within them? No, as born-again believers, they certainly did have the Holy Spirit dwelling within them. It means, rather, that they had not yet been baptized in the Holy Spirit like the 120 disciples experienced on the Day of Pentecost as recorded in Acts 2:4.

There are three observations that can be made from the Samaritan case. First, clearly this means there can be born-again believers who have not been baptized in the Holy Spirit. Second, observers can know when believers have not been baptized in the Holy Spirit (verses 14-16). And third, observers can know when believers have been baptized in the Holy Spirit (verses 17,18).

✎7. How did Philip and the apostles in Jerusalem know that these Samaritan Christians had not yet been filled with the Holy Spirit? *(Clue: They knew because of what the 120 believers experienced on the Day of Pentecost as recorded in Acts 2:4. And you will find the answer there likewise!)* What particular manifestation had occurred on the Day of Pentecost but had not yet occurred in the Samaritan believers?

_____

_____

Whereas, on the one hand, in Acts 8:14-16, the Christian community knew the Holy Spirit had not yet fallen on the Samaritan believers, on the other hand, according to the next two verses, they knew when He did fall on them. According to Acts 8:17,18, the apostles and Simon clearly and distinctly knew when these Samaritan Christians were baptized in the Holy Spirit. Obviously, there was some outwardly observable manifestation that occurred. What could it have been?

Admittedly, for some reason, Luke did not say what this manifestation was—at least, not in a straightforward statement. Thus, the question has often been asked: What was the manifestation that occurred on this occasion? While some contend that we cannot know; others, Pentecostals and non-Pentecostals, contend that in fact we can know.

F.F. Bruce discussed this incident in his classic commentary on Acts. Concerning the Samaritans' experience, he wrote: "The context leaves us in no doubt that their reception of the Spirit was attended by external manifestations such as had marked His descent on the earliest disciples at Pentecost" (F.F. Bruce, *Commentary on the Book of Acts.* Grand Rapids: Eerdmans, 1954, 181).

Among the "external manifestations" that "marked His descent ... at Pentecost" there was only one manifestation that occurred over again in Acts. For this reason, Bruce and other scholars concluded that the apostles and Simon heard the Samaritans speaking in tongues as the Spirit gave the utterance—just like the 120 believers on the Day of Pentecost.

Now turn to the third incident in Acts 10:44-47 and 11:15-17, the case of Cornelius and his household at Caesarea. The apostle Peter had been especially instructed by God to go to Caesarea to Cornelius, a Gentile, to explain to him about salvation in Jesus' name (Acts 10:1-22).

✎8. According to Acts 10:44, what happened to Cornelius and to others while Peter was explaining salvation in Jesus' name?

_____

✎9. How did Peter and the other Jewish Christians with him know that the Holy Spirit had fallen on these Gentile believers (Acts 10:45,46)?

_____

_____

Notice that this was the same outwardly observable manifestation that had occurred in the first incident of the baptism in the Holy Spirit on the Day of Pentecost (Acts 2:4).

✎ 10. When Peter returned to Jerusalem, he was asked to explain what had happened in Caesarea (Acts 11:15-17). In verse 15, Peter said the Holy Spirit "fell" or "came" on Cornelius. But how did he identify or describe that experience in verse 16?

_____

_____

Notice that the terminology here is the same as Jesus used in Acts 1:5 when He was telling His followers what they would experience on the coming Day of Pentecost. From this we can conclude that Cornelius and the others with him experienced the same experience as the 120 believers on the Day of Pentecost (Acts 2:4)—the baptism in the Holy Spirit—with the same manifestation—speaking in tongues.

The final incident in which Luke discussed believers' being baptized in the Holy Spirit was in Acts 19:1-6. When Paul came to Ephesus on his third missionary journey, he found a group of "disciples." Whether these "disciples" were already "Christians" by the time Paul found them or only "disciples" of John the Baptist is not really important to know. Certainly, by verse 5 they were born-again believers who were baptized by Paul in Christian baptism.

✎ 11. Paul explained the Holy Spirit to the Ephesian believers. What happened when he laid his hands on them after they were baptized in water (Acts 19:5,6)?

_____

✎ 12. What were the outwardly observable manifestations that occurred when the Ephesian believers were baptized in the Holy Spirit?

_____

As stated at the beginning of this lesson, Pentecostals believe that the baptism in the Holy Spirit experience is important. They believe it is important because Jesus indicated that this experience is the key to believers' being especially enabled by the Spirit to do the work of evangelism and discipleship. In light of the incidents we have studied above, Pentecostals also note that in every Spirit-baptism case recorded in the Bible, there were outwardly observable manifestations. Christians in the Book of Acts knew when believers had been baptized in the Holy Spirit. Further, Pentecostals observe that when Luke described these outwardly observable manifestations, there was one, and only one, manifestation that was common to all of the incidents. It was speaking in tongues as the Spirit gave the utterance.

Results Of Being Baptized In The Holy Spirit

One specific way the Holy Spirit enables believers to do the work of evangelism and discipleship is by giving them unusual boldness and wisdom. The Book of Acts is replete with many examples of this following the outpouring of the Spirit on the Day of Pentecost.

Immediately, on that very occasion (Acts 2:14ff), Peter took his stand, raised his voice, and declared the wisdom of God in Jesus Christ (see 1 Corinthians 1:18-24).

On many occasions, when the apostles were taken into custody, they manifested unusual wisdom and power concerning the things God was doing in Jesus Christ. The apostles were threatened, beaten, and imprisoned, but they continued to preach and minister for Christ with great boldness.

As previously stated, there are many examples of this in the Book of Acts, but we want to highlight a man named Stephen. His story is quite lengthy, covering from Acts 6:8 through 8:1. You may have already read this account, but if not, you may want to do so before moving on. This section will focus on Acts 6:8-10 and 7:54-60.

13. In Acts 6:8-10, what four terms did Luke use to describe Stephen?

_____

_____

Pentecostals contend that sometime before this Stephen had, no doubt, spoken in tongues as the Spirit gave the utterance when he was first filled with the Spirit. But in Acts 6, Luke described a believer who continued to be filled with the Spirit. Speaking in tongues is certainly a valid and very important experience, but the Bible admonishes us to be continually filled with the Spirit (Ephesians 5:18). When a believer continues to be filled with the Holy Spirit there should be continuing evidence of this in terms of His mighty works in and through that believer.

14. Look at Acts 6:9 and 7:54. Briefly state the results of the Spirit's anointing in the life of Stephen when he witnessed to the Jewish religious leaders. How did the Spirit help Stephen to be effective?

_____

_____

_____

_____

Stephen was so bold he was able to sacrificially give his life because of the power of the Spirit (Acts 7:59-60). Especially note his prayer in Acts 7:60 for those who stoned him to death.

Another specific way that the Spirit especially enables believers to do the work of evangelism and discipleship is by enabling them to work supernaturally in the "gifts" of the Spirit. These "gifts" are special abilities that the Spirit gives to believers in order to enable them to do extraordinary things.

Throughout the Book of Acts there are numerous cases of the Holy Spirit's manifesting a variety of gifts in and through the apostles and other believers. On the Day of Pentecost, immediately following the first outpouring of the Spirit, the gift of prophecy was manifested through Peter when he spoke to the multitude and 3,000 believed in Jesus as Savior (Acts 2:14-41). Later, when Peter and John went up to the temple to pray, the gifts of faith and healing were exercised and the lame man was made whole (Acts 3:1-10). There were many other occasions in Acts when the gift of healing was manifested. Likely, a word of knowledge was given through Peter when Ananias and Sapphira were stricken dead for lying to the Holy Spirit (Acts 5:1-10). The gift of a word of wisdom was manifested in the apostle

James when the first council of the Church met in Jerusalem to decide some issues relative to the Gentile believers (Acts 15:13-29). In verse 28 especially note their acknowledgment of the Spirit's role in their decision. These examples are only a few of the many incidents of specific gifts' being manifested in the Book of Acts.

In Romans 12:3-8, 1 Corinthians 12:4-12, and Ephesians 4:4-16 are listed many of the gifts of the Spirit. One should note, however, that even combined, these lists do not identify all of the many special gifts and abilities that the Spirit gives to believers or uses in and through believers from time to time.

✎15. **Read the passage in Romans 12:3-8 and list the seven gifts that Paul identified.**

_____

_____

_____

_____

_____

Remember that Paul did not intend this to be an exhaustive list. It was only suggestive of the variety of the gifts in the body of Christ.

✎16. **Look again closely at Romans 12:3 and restate Paul's one main purpose for writing about the gifts to the church at Rome.**

_____

_____

Anyone who has a special gift from God has no reason to be haughty or proud about it. Rather, they must remember that we each have our gifts only by the grace of God, and that other believers have great and important gifts as well.

✎17. **Read 1 Corinthians 12:4-12 and list the nine gifts Paul identified.**

_____

_____

_____

_____

_____

_____

_____

What was Paul's main point in 1 Corinthians 12:4-6? The King James Version uses the terms "diversities of" and "differences of." The New International Version says "different kinds of." The New American Standard Bible catches the idea very well with the phrase "varieties of." In other words, there are many kinds of gifts. In the verses that follow, Paul emphasized that all of these various gifts are important to the body of Christ.

✎ 18. Who did Paul say is the giver of all such gifts?

_____

One must read all of 1 Corinthians 12, 13, and 14 to fully understand Paul's reason for discussing the gifts of the Spirit. But for his short statement of the purpose for the manifestation of these gifts, see his last phrase in 1 Corinthians 14:5. The Holy Spirit manifests His gifts through individual believers for the edification of all persons. This is the reason Paul's great discourse on love is sandwiched in between his two definitive chapters on the manifestations of spiritual gifts.

The final passage on gifts to be considered is in Ephesians 4:4-16. Paul discussed some truly different kinds of "gifts" that some consider as offices and others as functions in the Church.

✎ 19. In Ephesians 4:4-6 here, Paul used the term "one" no less than seven times to emphasize the idea of unity or togetherness. Look again at the two previous passages on gifts that we have studied (Romans 12:3-8 and 1 Corinthians 12:4-12). Note in both of these passages where Paul expressed this same idea of unity or togetherness. Why do you think it was important to Paul to emphasize this idea every time he discussed special gifts?

_____

_____

_____

_____

_____

_____

✎ 20. List the five gifts or offices that Paul discussed in Ephesians 4:11.

_____

_____

_____

_____

_____

✎21. Notice in Ephesians 4:12-16 that the purpose of these gifts is to bring growth to the body of Christ and maturity to individual believers. Also, relate the function of leaders in verse 11 to the function of other believers in verse 12. How would you describe the relationship between these two groups as they work together to accomplish the goal of growth and maturity?

_____

_____

HISTORICAL PERSPECTIVE

From The Second Century Through The 19th Century

Our study above shows that the apostles and other early Christians witnessed and ministered in the full dynamics of the Spirit's special enablement. They were baptized in the Holy Spirit, and as a result they witnessed with boldness, they performed miraculous signs and wonders, and they won thousands to Jesus Christ.

Unfortunately, as we have seen in previous lessons, the nature of the Church changed significantly following the first century. The Church gradually deviated from the principle that Scripture is the final rule of faith and practice. This resulted in numerous doctrines and practices that were clearly not in keeping with the teachings of the New Testament. The pure doctrine of salvation by grace through faith was perverted. Other related truths such as personal relationship with God and the importance of living a holy life were also largely lost. Eventually, the Church was no longer characterized by the essential elements that we have observed above in our study of Acts in this lesson. That is, for the most part, from the second to the 19th century, the Church's life and ministry was not characterized by manifestations of spiritual gifts and the other dynamics of the Spirit's presence and power like it had been during the first century.

Turn Of 20th Century To The Present

In previous lessons we have already noted that during the last quarter of the 19th century and moving into the 20th century, some in the revivalism movement began to experience more of the Spirit's dynamics like those seen in Acts. They spoke in tongues, witnessed healings, and experienced other miracles and manifestations of the Spirit. These kinds of spiritual phenomena were occurring especially within the ranks of the Holiness Movement.

We previously identified a Holiness Movement minister, Charles F. Parham, as one of the first leaders of those who experienced these spiritual manifestations. In October 1900, he went to Topeka, Kansas, and started a Bible school for training young people to be ministers. Later that fall, Parham became interested in the biblical idea of "The baptism in the Holy Spirit."

In December, he instructed his students to study the New Testament to see if believers in New Testament times knew when they had been baptized in the Holy Spirit.

Parham's students discovered, as we have observed in our study above, that there are five incidents of believers' being baptized in the Holy Spirit recorded in the New Testament. Again, all of these are in the Book of Acts. Parham's students did a study of these incidents and reached two important conclusions. They concluded that, one, believers in New Testament times did know when they were baptized in the

Holy Spirit, because they spoke with tongues as the Spirit gave the utterance. And two, believers today could and should also have this same experience.

✎ **22. Notice that Parham's students reached these conclusions on the basis of their study of Scripture. And especially with regard to their second conclusion, apparently they applied the two principles that we have studied previously in studies 1 and 2. Review the first paragraph in each of these two lessons, and briefly state how these two principles are related to the second conclusion reached by Parham's students.** *(In both lessons the principle we are referring to is clearly stated in the last sentence of the first paragraph of the study.)*

_____

_____

Many believe the Pentecostal revival began and grew into a worldwide movement because Parham and others acted in accordance with these clear conclusions. Over a period of a few days, beginning on January 1, 1901, Parham and his students experienced the baptism in the Holy Spirit according to the Book of Acts pattern, speaking in tongues as the Spirit gave the utterance. Over the next five years the Pentecostal revival spread from Topeka, especially through Kansas, Missouri, Arkansas, Oklahoma, and Texas.

In Houston, Texas, Parham briefly established another Bible school where W.J. Seymour heard him teach about the baptism in the Holy Spirit and speaking in tongues. Seymour went to Los Angeles, California, where he opened a Pentecostal mission on Azusa Street. From 1906 to 1908, the Azusa Street Mission was the epicenter from which the Pentecostal revival eventually became a national and international movement.

SUMMARY

Pentecostals contend that the Book of Acts teaches the following points relative to the baptism in the Holy Spirit:
1. According to Jesus' statements, as recorded by Luke in Acts 1:8, the experience is given for the purpose of the bestowment of special power from the Spirit for witnessing.
2. In every recorded case of the baptism in the Holy Spirit in the Bible, there are outwardly observable manifestations immediately when the experience occurs.
3. In every recorded case where the writer Luke tells what the outwardly observable manifestations are, speaking in tongues is the only manifestation that is common to all of them.
4. Therefore, the New Testament teaches that observers can know when believers have had the initial experience of the baptism in the Holy Spirit because speaking in tongues is manifested.
5. The New Testament does not teach, in any place, that this experience was intended for only the Apostolic age; rather, the New Testament teaches that the special help of the Spirit will be needed for fully effective witnessing until the end of this age.
6. Therefore, in its teaching, the Book of Acts reveals a pattern that must be considered to be standard for doctrine and practice today.
7. Contemporary believers need to have the experience of the baptism in the Holy Spirit with speaking in tongues because this experience relates directly to the effectiveness of the Church in its efforts of evangelism and discipleship.

LET'S REVIEW

1. According to Acts 1:8 why did Jesus want His followers to be baptized in the Holy Spirit?

_____

2. The ministry of world evangelism and discipleship is still needed today because the task has not been completed. In fact, this effort must continue until Jesus returns. Are Christians today capable of adequately doing this important task simply with their own abilities and talents? Why or why not?

_____

_____

3. Identify the four incidents in the Book of Acts that reveal the pattern of outwardly observable manifestations that accompany the baptism in the Holy Spirit experience.

_____

_____

_____

_____

4. Why do Pentecostals believe that speaking in tongues as the Spirit gives the utterance is the initial evidence of the baptism in the Holy Spirit?

_____

5. Why did Parham's students conclude that the baptism in the Holy Spirit, accompanied with speaking in tongues, was an experience they should have?

_____

_____

6. Why do Pentecostals hold that it is important for all believers to be baptized in the Holy Spirit?

_____

_____

EVANGELICALISM:
EVANGELISM AND DISCIPLESHIP

From the beginning of the Pentecostal Movement, Pentecostals have considered themselves to be Bible-believing Christians squarely in the middle of the Protestant Reformation tradition. This means that Pentecostals are really a part of a larger movement known as Evangelicalism.

As we have seen in previous lessons, the Pentecostal Movement likewise has its roots in the First and Second Great Awakenings. Also, we have seen that Pentecostals hold strongly to the authority of Scripture and the other foundational doctrines of the Reformation. In this lesson, we will see how the Pentecostal Movement is part of Evangelicalism. Special attention will be given to the importance of evangelism and discipleship.

BIBLICAL BASIS

As Evangelicals, Pentecostals emphasize the importance of knowing sound, biblical doctrines and following through to be and act according to those doctrines.

✎1. In Matthew 15:7-9, Jesus indicated the importance of true doctrines when He taught that hypocrites follow

_____ .

(See the last part of verse 9 to fill in the blank.)

✎2. As Bible-believing Christians, the practice of the believers immediately following the Day of Pentecost, as seen in Acts 2:42, should be our example. Where do we find the apostles' doctrine or the apostles' teaching that is spoken of in this verse?

_____

_____

_____

After the Day of Pentecost, the apostles taught and preached over and over again what Jesus had taught them and what the Holy Spirit had shown them from Scripture about Jesus and the kingdom of God. After a few years the Holy Spirit inspired the apostles and their close associates to write down these teachings. The apostles' doctrine, referred to in Acts 2:42, has been preserved for us in the four Gospels and the Book of Acts. In the Epistles and the Book of Revelation, the Holy Spirit inspired these writers to further elaborate upon and illustrate these apostolic teachings.

✎3. In Ephesians 4:14 and Titus 1:9, what did Paul say knowing sound doctrines from Scripture prevents? Restate this idea in your own words.

_____

_____

_____

_____

Now look at the first part of Hebrews 13:9. In it the writer gave a clear admonition. Obviously, Christians can obey this admonition only when they know sound doctrine as taught in the Scriptures. As Evangelicals, Pentecostals also emphasize the importance of evangelism and discipleship.

4. Jesus' instructions in Matthew 28:19,20 are commonly known as The Great Commission. According to Matthew 28:16, Jesus was actually speaking to His 11 disciples (or apostles). Evangelicals consider these instructions to be directed to all Christians in all ages of the Church. Can you explain why? (Also, see Acts 4:12.)

_____

_____

_____

_____

Notice that Jesus' instructions obviously imply evangelism and explicitly emphasize discipleship. The task of the Church is to not only win converts, but also make disciples.

5. How would you describe the difference between converts and disciples? You may want to look up these two terms in a dictionary.

_____

_____

_____

_____

6. Why is John 3:16 often called the "Golden Text of the Bible"?

_____

_____

_____

_____

_____

7. Does whosoever really mean everyone?

_____

Pentecostals contend that the answer is certainly, "Yes." According to 2 Peter 3:9, Peter, one of Jesus' first leading apostles, clearly agreed.

8. Look at it this way. Whom did Peter say that God wants to perish?

_____

And, whom did Peter say that God wants to come to repentance?

_____

9. Romans 10:14,15 (NIV) is certainly one of the great passages on evangelism and discipleship in the Bible. Study this passage and notice that it includes five sentences—four questions and one declarative statement. Summarize this passage by restating the important point Paul made in each one of these five sentences.

_____

_____

_____

_____

_____

10. Read Acts 1:4-8. Briefly explain how the unique experience of baptism in the Holy Spirit is directly related to the task of evangelism and discipleship.

_____

_____

_____

_____

11. Explain why Pentecostals believe that it is still the Father's will for all believers to be baptized in the Holy Spirit. (If necessary, review the last paragraph of our study of Acts 1:4-8 in study 6. It is in the first part of the Biblical Basis section.)

_____

_____

_____

_____

Since God gives the special power of the Holy Spirit to believers to enable them to be effective witnesses, He must consider the task of evangelism and discipleship to be especially important!

HISTORICAL PERSPECTIVE

Early Decades Of The 20th Century

Pentecostals have often been misunderstood and considered to be strange or even heretical. It is true that, in comparison with much of Christianity, Pentecostals, from the beginning of the Movement, have had some rather unique doctrines and practices.

✎ 12. List some of the doctrines and practices that make Pentecostals unique when compared to other Christian groups.

_____

_____

_____

Because some Pentecostal doctrines and practices are different from other Christian groups, there has been a wide range of responses to Pentecostalism from various segments of Christianity. Some Holiness groups quickly accepted the doctrine and practice of speaking in tongues and became Pentecostal churches.

However, other Church groups reacted very negatively against the Pentecostal revival. These included other Holiness groups that rejected speaking in tongues, declaring it to be of the devil. Also, many Fundamentalists rejected the validity of Pentecostal experiences, saying that such manifestations were dispensationally only for the Apostolic Age. Most of the mainline denominational churches also took the position that Pentecostal experiences were not for the Church today. They simply tried to ignore the Pentecostal revival. Those groups that rejected the Pentecostal doctrines and practices ostracized those who spoke in tongues.

Because of these negative reactions, the Pentecostal Movement could have been destroyed, like previous, similar movements. A detailed study of Church history reveals there were several Pentecostal/Charismatic type movements from the second to the 19th centuries. Invariably, other Christians considered members of these movements to be strange and extreme. Unfortunately, these Pentecostal/Charismatic type groups usually responded by becoming more fanatical and then drifting into heresies of various kinds. Consequently, these movements were relatively short lived, being destroyed by alienation and extremes.

✎ 13. In study 5, we identified some Holiness groups that accepted speaking in tongues and became Pentecostal early in the 20th century. Can you remember some of these and list them here?

_____

_____

_____

_____

✑14. Explain why alienation, heresies and other extremes often destroy Christian groups.

_____

_____

_____

_____

_____

In the early years of the contemporary Pentecostal Movement, it appeared that history might be repeated. Significant parts of the Church world rejected the doctrines and practices of the Pentecostals and attempted to brand them as fanatics and heretics. Yet Pentecostals continued to insist that Scripture was their final rule for faith and practice. According to the Book of Acts, the first century Church was also characterized by similar doctrines and practices. Pentecostals contended these doctrines and practices were clearly biblical. Everything they taught, including speaking in tongues, was according to Scripture.

✑15. (TRUE/FALSE) Those who rejected the doctrines and practices of the Pentecostals did so more on the basis of historical considerations than on an objective consideration of Scripture.

_____

Those who rejected Pentecostalism observed that speaking in tongues and other manifestations of spiritual gifts were not commonly practiced throughout the Church from the second through the 19th centuries. Regardless of biblical evidence, they concluded that these manifestations were not for the contemporary Church.

During the first four decades of the 20th century, these Christian groups continued to deny the validity of Pentecostal experiences. They contended that speaking in tongues and other manifestations of the spiritual gifts were only for the Apostolic Age.

After 1940

In 1941, when Fundamentalist leaders formed the American Council of Christian Churches, they intentionally did not invite Pentecostals to be a part. Evangelicals, however, began to recognize the impressive accomplishments of Pentecostals in such areas as Sunday school literature and world missions. Eventually, they acknowledged the fact Pentecostals were also evangelical.

In 1942, Evangelical leaders invited the Assemblies of God and other Pentecostals to join in forming the National Association of Evangelicals. Since then Pentecostals have been visible and active participants, both as members and leaders in various areas of this growing association. Fundamentalists, however, have continued to resist Pentecostal doctrines and practices.

✎ 16. On the basis of the two paragraphs above, make your own observations about the strength and duration of Fundamentalism's opposition to Pentecostals in comparison to that of Evangelicals.

_____

_____

_____

_____

_____

_____

SUMMARY

Pentecostals are evangelical. And like other Evangelicals, they believe it is very important for all Christians to know sound doctrines that are developed from Scripture and to conduct their lives accordingly. Pentecostals also believe that all Christians should share their faith and endeavor to lead others to Jesus Christ. Pentecostals share the evangelical emphasis on evangelism and discipleship, but also hold that the experience of baptism in the Holy Spirit, with speaking in tongues, is for all believers in the Church. Pentecostals believe that, according to Acts 1:4-8, this experience is provided by God to empower believers to be more effective in evangelism and discipleship.

Because speaking in tongues and manifestations of other spiritual gifts were not common for many centuries, Pentecostal doctrines and practices have often seemed strange to others in the Church. But Pentecostals note that these doctrines and practices are taught in Scripture. Since the Bible is the final rule for faith and practices, and since God desires for the Church to be empowered by the Spirit until the end of this age, these experiences should have been the norm through all the Church Age.

Pentecostals have provided a sustained thrust on the importance of Spiritual manifestations. Unfortunately, some Pentecostals and Charismatics have allowed some extreme, questionable doctrines and practices. For the most part, however, the Pentecostal Movement has maintained a balanced Evangelical stance. Therefore, the movement has survived and developed into a major force in world-wide evangelism and discipleship.

LET'S REVIEW

1. List some Scriptures that emphasize the importance of knowing and following sound, biblical doctrines. Also list some Scriptures that emphasize evangelism and discipleship.

_____

_____

2. How is being a Christian disciple different from simply being a Christian convert? Why do Pentecostals and other Evangelicals emphasize the importance of being not only a convert but also a disciple?

_____

_____

_____

3. Why do Pentecostals associate the experience of baptism in the Holy Spirit with the task of evangelism and discipleship? *(You may want to review Acts 1:4,8.)*

_____

_____

_____

4. Why have some Christian groups responded negatively against Pentecostal doctrines and practices?

_____

_____

_____

5. In this study we discussed two reasons why Pentecostals contend that they are Evangelicals—two important, central things that Evangelicals and Pentecostals both emphasize. Can you identify them? *(For review look at the very first sentence under the Biblical Basis section and the last sentence right before item 4 in the Biblical Basis section.)*

_____

_____

EVANGELICALISM: ESCHATOLOGY

We have shown that Pentecostals are Bible-believing Christians, being part of a larger movement known as Evangelicalism. In the previous lesson we highlighted key evangelical doctrines and practices such as the authority of Scripture, personal conversion through Jesus Christ, and the task of evangelism and discipleship.

In this final lesson, we will study another important group of doctrines that Pentecostalism draws from its Evangelical roots. Collectively, these doctrines are often referred to as Eschatology. They deal with how and when God will bring to final completion His plans of full redemption and restoration. This lesson features "Christ's Second Coming," "Christ's Millennial Reign," and "The Perfect Eternal Age."

Christ's Second Coming

The doctrine of the second coming of Jesus Christ is one of the cardinal doctrines of Pentecostal belief. Yet it is often misunderstood because there are many passages of Scripture that describe this event in seemingly contradictory ways. Some verses state that believers will be caught up with Christ in the air; in others, the saints are coming back with Christ. Some declare that believers will be completely changed, while others indicate that they have already been changed when Christ returns. However, if all of the passages dealing with the Second Coming are studied and outlined, then the events associated with this wonderful event become clear. This section will help you understand what the Rapture is, and when Christ will return to earth to defeat the armies of Satan and set up His millennial kingdom.

The Rapture

1. Read John 14:3. What does Jesus say He will do?

_____

_____

The hope of Jesus' return is based upon Jesus' own promise to believers. Jesus' second coming is as sure as the fact of His first coming.

2. Briefly state the occasion, i.e., the historical situation, of Acts 1:9-11.

_____

_____

_____

We do not know if the two men in white were Old Testament saints or angelic beings. But their message to those bewildered followers of Jesus was clear: This Jesus *WILL* come back! In John 14:3 we have Jesus' own promise of His return and in Acts 1:9-11 we have two more witnesses to the same truth.

Read 1 Thessalonians 4:15-17. First, notice Paul repeated the promise that Jesus will come back. Second, notice he spoke about believers who will have already died and believers who will still be alive at that time.

3. What did Paul say will happen to believers who will have already died when Jesus returns? To believers who are still alive?

_____

_____

First Thessalonians 4:15-17 is a key Scripture on the doctrine of believers' resurrection, yet there are others. In 1 Corinthians 15:12-57, Paul elaborated further on the resurrection of believers.

✎ **4. Briefly describe what will happen to believers when Jesus returns (1 Corinthians 15:50-57).**

_____

_____

_____

Pentecostals commonly refer to this event as the rapture of the Church. Commentators have often noted that the term *rapture* is not found in the Bible. But clearly the truth of the Rapture is communicated by Paul's words *caught up* in 1 Thessalonians 4:17. (Note: The term *rapture* is derived from the Latin word for "caught up.")

The Second Advent

Read Revelation 19:11-19. Notice that someone comes from heaven (verse 11) to the earth (verse 19) riding on a white horse. Also notice that this someone is called Faithful and True (verse 11), The Word of God (verse 13), and King of kings and Lord of lords (verse 16). Obviously, this someone is Jesus Christ. Clearly, John the Revelator was also talking about Jesus' return to the earth.

✎ **5. In verse 14: (a.) whom did John say comes with Jesus, (b.) where do they come from, and (c.) what are they wearing?**

a._____

b. _____

c._____

The terminology fine linen, white and clean, is significant because it clearly identifies these armies from heaven as redeemed saints.

Notice in the event described by Paul in 1 Thessalonians 4:15-17, the redeemed go up to meet the Lord in the air. But in the event described in Revelation 19:11-19, the redeemed come down with Jesus from heaven to earth. Yet both of these events are part of the second coming of Jesus.

It is clear there are two aspects to the Second Coming. The first is often called the Rapture, derived from Paul's terminology in 1 Thessalonians 4:17. In this aspect, Jesus comes only in the clouds and the redeemed are caught up to meet Him in the air.

To identify the second aspect of Christ's second coming, we will use the terminology Second Advent. This term indicates, as seen in Revelation 19:11-19, that Jesus comes all the way back to the earth. Also, note that the redeemed come with Him from heaven.

Christ's Millennial Reign

We studied about the second advent of Jesus in Revelation 19:11-19. Look again at verse 19 and also read verses 20 and 21. At the Second Advent, Jesus defeats the forces of evil led by the beast and false prophet. Many believe this same battle is spoken of by John in Revelation 16:13-16. Because of the location identified in verse 16, this battle is often referred to as the Battle of Armageddon. After this battle, the Lord sets up His kingdom on earth. This kingdom is often referred to as the millennial reign of Christ.

Read Revelation 20:1-6. The beginning of verse 1 means the events here immediately follow the events in Revelation 19:11-21.

6. What happens to Satan at this time and for how long?

_____

_____

7. According to Revelation 20:4-6, what are Jesus Christ and the redeemed doing during this 1,000-year period?

_____

_____

This reign of Christ on earth is often called the millennial reign of Christ, the millennial kingdom of Christ, or simply the Millennium. The term *millennium* is derived from Latin, meaning 1,000 years. Pentecostals usually believe this kingdom of Christ will be not only a spiritual kingdom but also a literal kingdom in which Christ will reign as an actual king here on the earth.

Read Isaiah 11:1-9. Isaiah prophesied to God's people during the reigns of kings Uzziah, Jotham, Ahaz, and Hezekiah. He prophesied during the decades just prior to when the Babylonians overpowered Judah and took away the kingdom (2 Kings 25). Isaiah prophesied that because of the Israelites' sin and disobedience, God would allow the Babylonians to take them into captivity. He also prophesied that God would still be with His people, and in the future would totally restore His kingdom. In spite of their failures, God would ultimately fulfill His original plan to use the seed of Abraham to bring redemption to all peoples of the earth.

Evangelical Bible scholars commonly agree that, even to this day, the things prophesied about in Isaiah 11:1-9 have not yet been fulfilled. That is, the things spoken of in this passage have not yet occurred.

8. Look through Isaiah 11:1-9 again. Make a list of all the conditions that have not yet existed that Isaiah said will exist someday in the future.

_____

_____

_____

Evangelical scholars believe that Isaiah 11:1-9 describes conditions of justice and peace that will exist during Jesus' millennial reign on earth as King of kings and Lord of lords. Even the animals will exist in peace with each other and with human beings.

Now read Micah 4:3. This is another place scholars believe the prophet is speaking of conditions during Jesus' peaceful millennial kingdom on earth.

9. What condition is pictured by Micah's contrast between plowshares and pruning hooks on the one hand, and spears and swords on the other? What condition exists in many places in the world today but will not exist at all during the Millennium?

_____

_____

_____

_____

_____

Jesus Christ's millennial reign will be a time of righteous justice and total peace all over the earth. And as Isaiah 11:9 says, the earth will be full of the knowledge of the Lord. Everyone will experience God's infinite goodness first-hand.

Satan will be bound during this entire thousand-year period (Revelation 20:1-3), so he will not be able to deceive nor tempt anyone. Since everyone will have full knowledge of the Lord, there will be no reason to not love and serve God fully. Read Revelation 20:7-10. Note that after the thousand years of Jesus' reign, Satan is released.

10. What does Satan immediately begin to do after he is released?

_____

_____

11. How do multitudes of people, who experienced the perfect righteousness and peace of God during Jesus' reign on earth, respond to Satan's activities at this time?

_____

_____

_____

_____

✎ 12. What, then, does the Millennium prove about the claim of those who say they would gladly serve God if they could only see Him, and thereby know He is real?

_____

_____

_____

_____

According to Revelation 20:8, at the end of the Millennium another battle occurs between God and Satan. Because of the terminology used by John in this verse, this battle is often referred to as the Battle of Gog and Magog.

✎ 13. Read Revelation 20:10-15. What finally happens to Satan and those who follow him?

_____

_____

_____

The Perfect Eternal Age

The last half of Revelation 20 tells how that, at the end of the Millennium, God will finally deal with all who oppose Him. Revelation 21 and 22 describe the new, perfect, eternal age God will prepare for all who have accepted His plan of redemption through Jesus Christ. The apostle Peter prophesied concerning this change—when this present age will end and a new age will begin. Read this in 2 Peter 3:10-13.

✎ 14. How did Peter say this present age will end? What did he recommend with regard to how we should live?

_____

_____

_____

_____

✎ 15. What did Peter say will come after the present heavens and earth are destroyed?

_____

_____

Read Revelation 21:1-5. Notice John wrote about the same thing as Peter—the passing away of this present heaven and earth and the coming of a new heaven and earth.

✎ 16. Using Revelation 21:3,4, describe some of the characteristics of the perfect age that will come.

_____

_____

_____

✎ 17. According to Revelation 21:5, who makes these promises concerning this coming age? How certain can we be that these things will actually come?

_____

_____

_____

The rest of Revelation 21 and first half of Revelation 22 describe the New Jerusalem, the river of life, and the tree of life that will be central to this new, perfect age.

✎ 18. Summarize the promises given in Revelation 21:27 and 22:3.

_____

_____

_____

_____

Praise God! He will finally deliver us from all that is evil and of the curse! However, according to the last part of Revelation 21:27, the perfect eternal age is prepared for only those whose names are written in the Lamb's Book of Life. Only those who have accepted Jesus Christ as their personal Savior will have their names written there. Only they will be allowed to enter into that perfect eternal age with God.

We have limited our study to the basic, biblical teachings on some special areas of Eschatology. For many centuries, the Church's teachings on these topics, generally speaking, were not detailed beyond these basic points. In recent centuries, however, these doctrines have been developed in more detail.

To the present, the basic biblical teachings that we studied are still agreed upon commonly by Evangelicals. But when details of these doctrines are considered, there are some variations among Evangelicals and Pentecostals. These are especially notable in the doctrines of the Second Coming and the Millennium

HISTORICAL PERSPECTIVE

Second Coming Views

During the 19th and 20th centuries, variations in the doctrine of the second coming of Christ developed among Evangelicals. The most significant of these variations are related to the two aspects that we have already studied of the Second Coming: first the Rapture described by Paul in 1 Thessalonians 4:15-17, and second, the Second Advent pictured by John in Revelation 19:11-16. Together, these two aspects comprise the Second Coming.

The variations in this doctrine also center around the question of when the Rapture will occur in relationship to a special time called the Great Tribulation. This is a special seven-year period just prior to the Millennium. During this time God's wrath will be poured out upon the earth toward those who insist upon rebelling against Him.

✎ 19. Read about the Great Tribulation in the following Scripture passages: Daniel 9:24-27; 11:31-33; Matthew 24:15-21; Jeremiah 30:7; and Revelation 13-18. List some things that will characterize the Great Tribulation.

_____

_____

_____

_____

_____

_____

There are three basic views concerning the relationship of the Rapture to the Great Tribulation. Some Evangelicals and Pentecostals take the position the Rapture will occur just before the Great Tribulation. This view is call Pretribulationism. Others take the position the Rapture will occur in the middle of the Great Tribulation. This view is called Midtribulationism. Still others take the position the Rapture will occur at the end of the Great Tribulation. This view is called Posttribulationism.

It is important to note the relationship of the Rapture to the Second Advent in these three views. In Pretribulationism, the Rapture occurs at the beginning of the Great Tribulation, and the Second Advent occurs at the end of the Great Tribulation, with seven years between them. In Midtribulationism, the Rapture occurs in the middle of the Great Tribulation, and the Second Advent occurs at the end of the Great Tribulation, with three and one-half years between them. In Posttribulationism, the Rapture and Second Advent both occur at the end of the Great Tribulation, with practically no lapse of time between.

Notice in all three of these views, the Second Advent occurs at the end of the Great Tribulation. There is agreement on that point. But with regard to when the Rapture occurs, some Pentecostals hold to the Pretribulation view, while others hold to the Midtribulation or Posttribulation views.

For two particular reasons, however, many Pentecostal groups prefer to hold to the Pretribulation Rapture view. One reason has to do with God's pouring out His wrath upon the earth toward those who have insisted upon rebelling against His grace. Those who hold the Pretribulation view believe God will take those who have received His gracious plan of salvation out of the earth before the Great Tribulation. This view states that the righteous will not suffer God's wrath (see 1 Thessalonians 5:9).

Another reason why some hold strongly to the Pretribulation view has to do with the belief in the imminent return of Christ.

20. Look up the term *imminent* in a dictionary and write down the first definition given there.

_____

_____

_____

Caution: The term *imminent* must not be confused with the term *immanent*. Whereas, *immanent* means "close with," while *imminent* (the idea we are dealing with) means "about to happen."

The doctrine of the imminent return of Christ means that His return will soon occur (see Revelation 3:11; 22:7,12,20).

Those who hold the Pretribulation view believe the imminent return of Christ means He can return at any time. There is nothing that must occur before Christ returns to appear in the clouds. Pretribulationists note that in the Midtribulation and Posttribulation Rapture views, some or all of the Great Tribulation must occur before Christ returns. They contend that if either of these views is correct, then Christ cannot return now. They conclude that only the Pretribulation Rapture view allows for belief in the imminent return of Christ.

Millennialism Views

There are also variations in the doctrine of the Millennium. These can be grouped into three main classifications: *Pre*millennialism, *Post*millennialism, and *A*millennialism.

Premillennialism teaches that there will not be any time of significant peace on the earth until Jesus returns to establish His kingdom here. In this view, Jesus must come back before the Millennium can begin. This is the reason for the prefix *pre*, meaning before. This view also teaches that Christ's kingdom will be not only a spiritual kingdom, but also a literal kingdom in which Jesus will reign as an actual king here on the earth. Believers from all ages will return and rule with Christ during this thousand-year period.

Postmillennialism teaches that the Church will be increasingly successful in propagating the gospel. Gradually, good will overcome evil, and eventually peace will be established throughout the earth. In this view the kingdom of God will be established by the Church's propagation of the gospel. After the gospel has prevailed, Christ will return to receive His kingdom. This is the reason for the prefix *post*, meaning after.

✎ 21. One significant difference between these two views is the timing of Jesus' return. Can you identify some other significant differences?

_____

_____

Amillennialism teaches that Christ's kingdom on earth is only a spiritual reign in the hearts and lives of believers, and is already established and growing. In this view, Jesus does not and will not have a literal 1,000-year reign here on the earth. This is the reason for the prefix *a*, meaning no. In Amillennialism, most Scriptures on the kingdom of God are taken figuratively rather than literally.

✎ 22. Why do most Pentecostals reject the Amillennial idea of the reign of Christ?

_____

_____

According to R.G. Clouse, the predominate concept of the earliest millennial teaching was the idea that God would establish His kingdom on earth through a series of unusual, dramatic events. These events included the coming of Daniel's Son of Man (Daniel 7:13). The Church held that the books of Daniel and Revelation taught these events. This view, which has been called historic premillennialism, was the prevailing view during the first three centuries of the Christian era.

Later, near the beginning of the fifth century, Augustine, Bishop of Hippo, led the way in developing the Amillennial view. By then, the allegorical (figurative) method had become a predominate way of understanding the Bible. Augustine applied the allegorical method of interpretation to Scriptures on the kingdom of God. By doing so, he developed the Amillennial view, which then prevailed throughout the Medieval period of the Church and continued into the Reformation. Nevertheless, the Reformers instituted changes that laid the foundation for renewal of the Premillennial view. The most important of these changes was the Reformer's rejection of the allegorical method in favor of the literal interpretation of Scripture.

✎ 23. Augustine's allegorical method of interpretation is also called *allegorization* or *allegorizing*. These terms refer to a method of understanding the Bible. *Allegory*, on the other hand, is a common literary technique. Allegorization and allegorizing are related to, but are not the same as, the technique of allegory. Look up these words in a dictionary. Identify the difference between allegorization and allegorizing, and allegory.

_____

_____

_____

Millennial teachings became especially varied following the Protestant Reformation. With some variations, Premillennialism was revived, especially during the 17th century. Postmillennial views first grew out of the 18th century Enlightenment. Amillennialism was also restored during that century. Premillennialism waned during the 18th century; but it once again became especially popular during the 19th century.

Most Pentecostal groups strongly favor the Premillennial view of Christ's reign here on earth. They believe this view flows most naturally from a straightforward, normal interpretation of Scripture. When the materials on the Millennium are understood in the way the biblical authors intended, the Premillennial position is clearly derived.

They recognize that there is, of course, considerable figurative language used to describe various aspects of the Millennium. But this figurative language describes a real, literal time when Jesus will reign as an actual king here on earth. For example, most Pentecostals believe there is no reason for the 1,000 years identified by John in Revelation 20:1-6 to be understood only figuratively or symbolically, so they reject the Amillennial view.

Also, most Pentecostals reject the Postmillennial view. Again, they submit that the Premillennial view flows most clearly out of normal interpretation of Scripture. More specifically, they contend the Postmillennial view contradicts such Scriptures as Matthew 24:3-12; 2 Timothy 3:1-5; 1 Thessalonians 5:1-3; and 2 Peter 3:3,4. In Matthew 24:3-12, Jesus himself said that in the last days lawlessness will increase, not decrease as the Postmillennial view suggests. In 2 Timothy 3:1, Paul said the last days will be especially difficult times. According to 1 Thessalonians 5:3, Paul said men may think peace is at hand, but sudden destruction is coming. Peter expressed the same view in 2 Peter 3:1-13. Pentecostals who hold to the Premillennial view contend that the world will not get better and better before Jesus returns (as the Postmillennial view holds). Rather, the only way for peace to be established on earth is for Jesus to literally return and establish His kingdom.

SUMMARY

Pentecostals, along with other Evangelicals, believe God will eventually complete His full plan of redemption and restoration. Satan and all evil will be defeated, and God will establish perfect peace and righteousness for all eternity. At the end of this present age, Jesus will return as promised in Acts 1:9-11 and 1 Thessalonians 4:17. All the redeemed—both those who have already died and those who remain alive at the time—will be caught up to meet Him in the air, as Paul described in 1 Thessalonians 4:15-17. This event, called the rapture of the Church, is the first part of Christ's second coming. Pentecostals traditionally tend to believe this event will occur before, rather than during or after the Great Tribulation period of seven years.

Following the Great Tribulation, believers will rule with Christ in His millennial kingdom. Most Pentecostals believe Jesus will physically come back to earth with the saints of all ages to rule in a literal kingdom. This return is called the Second Advent. It is the second and concluding part of the second coming of Christ, and marks the beginning of the millennial reign of Christ. Most Pentecostals also believe this Kingdom will last for a literal 1,000 years as stated in Revelation 20:1-6. During this time Jesus will reign as King and will establish genuine peace and true righteousness.

After the Millennium, God himself will come down to dwell eternally in a new heaven and earth that He will create. Satan, along with all who have continued in rebellion with him, will be cast into outer darkness forever. Nothing evil or in any way contrary to God will ever enter the eternal, perfect age. Believers, whose names are written in the Lamb's Book of Life, will live forever in the presence of God.

LET'S REVIEW

1. How do we know that Jesus will return to this earth someday? What Scriptures do we have for this promise?

_____

_____

2. We have seen that the Bible pictures two aspects to the second coming of Christ. What aspect of the Second Coming is pictured by Paul in 1 Thessalonians 4:15-17?

_____

_____

3. What are the two main reasons many Pentecostals believe the Rapture will occur before the Great Tribulation?
(For review, see Historical Perspective section, page 66.)

1 _____

2 _____

4. What aspect of Christ's second coming is pictured by John in Revelation 19:11-19?

_____

_____

5. What will be the most important characteristics of Christ's millennial kingdom? What Scriptures tell us about this?

_____

_____

6. We studied three basic millennial views. Which one of these do most Pentecostals believe and why?
(For review, see Historical Perspective section, page 66.)

_____

_____

Additional titles in the
SPIRITUAL *Discovery* SERIES

The Foundations Track

SG 02-0104
LG 02-0204

A New Way Of Life by Robert L. Brandt introduces new converts to the major practices and beliefs of the Pentecostal/Charismatic community. The biblical basis of salvation, water baptism, communion, the baptism in the Holy Spirit, church membership, stewardship, and evangelism are discussed. Additional studies detail ways to become an effective Christian through the discipline of Bible reading and prayer, and developing daily standards of conduct.

SG 02-0111
LG 02-0211

Baptized In The Spirit by Frank M. Boyd is an updated and reformatted version of a Pentecostal classic. Users of this title will come to understand the nature of the Holy Spirit, His ministry, the biblical basis for the baptism in the Holy Spirit, the initial evidence, how to receive, means of staying full, and the various gifts of the Spirit and their proper usage.

SG 02-0113
LG 02-0213

A Heart For The Lost by Robert L. Brandt will motivate individuals to prepare for the task of evangelizing. Brandt leads individuals into an exploration of the basis of evangelism, and then proposes a biblical standard for performing the task. Those who use *A Heart For The Lost* will discover that evangelism is not an activity to be feared, but a natural extension of one's Christian experience.

SG 02-0107
LG 02-0207

Spiritual Devotion by Dr. Nathan H. Nelson explores the art and discipline of developing one's spiritual relationship to God. This study challenges individuals to go beyond mechanical devotional routine toward intimacy with their God. Those who seek a deeper spiritual devotion will find this title refreshing, insightful, and rewarding.

SG 02-0118
LG 02-0218

Biblical Foundations by Donald F. Johns explores 13 commonly held Pentecostal beliefs and leads the learner into an understanding of the biblical basis for each. Topics include salvation, water baptism, and the baptism in the Holy Spirit.

SG 02-0123
LG 02-0223

Living By The Spirit by Lorraine Mastrorio introduces readers to the Spirit baptism experience, describes the fruit of the Spirit, and encourages them to allow God to use them through the supernatural and ministry gifts. It provides direction for Pentecostal believers in their quest to live a Spirit-led lifestyle.

SG 02-0126
LG 02-0226

Missions: Home And Abroad by Delmer Guynes is a challenge to the Church throughout the world to be missions-minded. Jesus' Great Commission is a command to every believer and to every church—all must be actively involved in missions efforts both in their homeland as well as in foreign countries. Guynes explores the means, the call, the resources, and the patterns for the missions task God has presented His Church.

Additional titles in the
SPIRITUAL *Discovery* SERIES

The Life Issues Track

Facing Midlife Challenges by Dr. Raymond T. Brock explores the transitions of life, personal fulfillment, physical changes, sexual adjustments, mortality, and more. This book is good for those in the midst of midlife or approaching it.

SG 02-0115
LG 02-0215

One For The Lord by Dr. Earl G. Creps helps singles examine their position in the world, their place in the Church, and their relationship to God. Learners will be encouraged to discover God's purpose and fulfillment in their lives.

SG 02-0117
LG 02-0217

Parenting: The Early Years by Kay E. Marchand is designed to address issues confronted by new parents—prenatal through preschool. Various aspects of parenting including making preparations for a newborn, introducing a child to Jesus, proper nutrition, discipline, learning stages, developmental stages, and communication patterns are explored.

SG 02-0106
LG 02-0206

Parenting The Elementary Child by Dr. Raymond T. Brock addresses developmental stages, discipline techniques, developing a spiritual climate in the home, the birthing order, financial stress, and intimacy challenges faced by parents during this ever-changing time. Additional studies focus on the unique challenges of the one-parent family, the blended family, the traditional family, and families with exceptional children.

SG 02-0109
LG 02-0209

Christians In The Workplace by Roberta Bonnici exhorts the believer to worship God in the workplace through their Christian conduct and attitude toward those with whom they work. Bonnici offers practical advice which will help Christians as they encounter challenges to their faith and temptations to compromise their personal values. Those who use this book will understand the origin of work and its value.

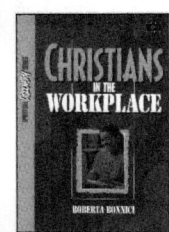

SG 02-0127
LG 02-0227

Building Healthy Marriages by Terry Bryant challenges husbands and wives to apply biblical truths to the God-ordained relationship of marriage. Bryant offers practical insights on such topics as what it means to leave and cleave, how two people can truly achieve oneness, how to be a person of commitment, how to employ proper and effective communication, and what it means to grow spiritually as a couple

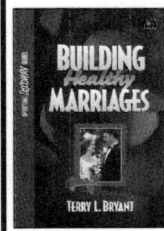

SG 02-0129
LG 02-0229

Stepparenting by Dr. Billie Davis gives much-needed help concerning an increasingly common situation in contemporary society. Dr. Davis' insights and suggestions will help those who face this situation to plan and execute proper relations within their stepfamily. Dr. Davis provides hope for those who feel overwhelmed by encouraging them to walk step-by-step along this challenging path in the strength and power of the Holy Spirit.

SG 02-0130
LG 02-0230

Additional titles in the
SPIRITUAL *Discovery* SERIES

The Book Study Track

SG 02-0108
LG 02-0208

How To Study The Bible by G. Raymond Carlson introduces the learner to the background of our present Bible, rationale for studying the biblical text, and techniques to enrich the believer's Bible study experience. Users will explore the inductive method of Bible study, topical study procedures, biographical studies, word studies, and the synthetic method of Bible study.

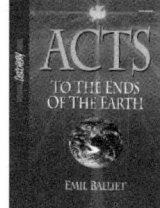

SG 02-0105
LG 02-0205

Bible Prophecy by Dr. Stanley M. Horton involves the learner in an investigation of end-time events. They will discover the purpose of prophecy, methods of interpretation, and specific events which the Bible clearly predicts. ***Bible Prophecy*** demystifies prophecy and encourages learners to live with expectancy and faithfulness as they await Christ's coming.

SG 02-0112
LG 02-0212

Acts: To The Ends Of The Earth by Emil Balliet is an inductive study designed to guide the learner toward an understanding of the historical context and theological content of the Book of Acts. Those who engage in this study will be challenged to discover and apply eternal principles introduced by the Holy Spirit through the First Century Church.

SG 02-0116
LG 02-0216

Letters To Corinth by Dr. Charles Harris engages the learner in an exegetical examination of the letters of 1 and 2 Corinthians. This series of studies provide answers to various issues faced by local churches throughout history including disunity, immorality, spiritual excess, faulty theology, suffering, and stewardship.

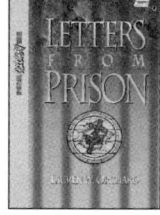

SG 02-0121
LG 02-0221

Letters From Prison by Lauren W. Orchard examines Paul's letters to the churches of Ephesus, Colosse, and Philippi and to Philemon. It shares God's design for a personal relationship with God and with those whom believers fellowship.

SG 02-0119
LG 02-0219

Romans by G. Raymond Carlson examines Paul's letter to the Romans introducing learners to many of the theological concepts vital to the Christian experience such as original sin, sanctification, justification, Redemption, and the Atonement.

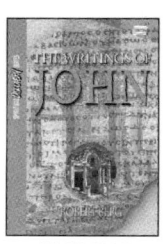

SG 02-0115
LG 02-0215

Writings of John by Robert Berg sheds new light on the time and culture in which these vital books of the Bible were written. Dr. Robert Berg's unique approach will give you a deeper understanding of the Gospel of John as well as insight into First, Second, and Third John. The Writings Of John leads readers into the Scriptures to learn Who the Word of God is, how Jesus is just like His Father, what the Holy Spirit has been sent to accomplish, how to remain in Christ, when Jesus accomplished His earthly mission, and how to know who "true" Christians are.

Additional titles in the
SPIRITUAL *Discovery* SERIES

The Critical Concerns Track

Sanctity Of Life by Michael H. Clarensau focuses on the biblical perspective regarding current life issues facing today's Church. Issues examined include the value of life, the power of death, abortion, birth control, genetic engineering, suicide, murder, capital punishment, genocide, and euthanasia.

SG 02-0115
LG 02-0215

Combating The Darkness by John T. Maempa is designed to equip the believer to recognize and respond appropriately to spiritual attacks. Maempa avoids sensationalism by directing the learner to biblical passages that provide a firm foundation on which to stand strong in the midst of spiritual warfare.

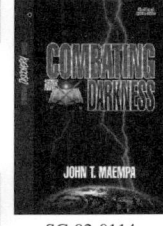

SG 02-0114
LG 02-0214

Journey To Integrity by Michael H. Clarensau proclaims the importance of character in the Christian's life. Clarensau recognizes integrity is a process and provides a plan which, if followed, will lead to the user's desired destination.

SG 02-0120
LG 02-0220

Recovery For Codependency by Steven E. Stiles is a step-by-step path to recovery from negative behaviors and addictions. It is for those personally struggling with an addictive behavior or assisting someone else in his or her struggle.

SG 02-0122
LG 02-0222

Managing Stress Through Positive Christian Living by Paul A. Lee and Mark & Carole Ryan explains that stress does not have to control our lives. By enriching our relationship with God, we can learn to change our responses and gain control over stress.

SG 02-0125
LG 02-0225

In Search Of Truth by Paul W. Smith, Clancy P. Hayes, and Kerry D. McRoberts provides an overview of the distinctions between Christianity and Judaism, Mormonism, Islam, Atheism, Spiritism, the New Age Movement, and other groups. It will help Christians respond appropriately to individuals within these groups.

SG 02-0124
LG 02-0224

Music God Likes by Dr. Joseph Nicholson examines the wide variety of musical styles employed by the Church today. He encourages his readers to expand their musical options and appreciate musical styles they may have previously avoided in both personal and corporate worship.

SG 02-0128
LG 02-0228